Effective HRM Practices

Effective HRM Practices

Perspectives on Engineering Education in India

V R K Prasad

Viva Books

New Delhi | Mumbai | Chennai | Kolkata | Bengaluru | Hyderabad | Kochi | Guwahati

Publisher's note

Every possible effort has been made to ensure that the information contained in this book is accurate at the time of going to press, and the publisher and author cannot accept responsibility for any errors or omissions, however caused. No responsibility for loss or damage occasioned to any person acting, or refraining from action, as a result of the material in this publication can be accepted by the editor, the publisher or the author.

Every effort has been made to trace the owners of copyright material used in this book. The author and the publisher will be grateful for any omission brought to their notice for ack.nowledgment in the future editions of the book.

First Published 2013
Reprinted 2015, 2018, 2023

Viva Books Private Limited

- 4737/23, Ansari Road, Daryaganj, New Delhi 110 002
  Tel. 42242200, 23258325, 23283121, Email: vivadelhi@vivagroupindia.in
- 76, Service Industries, Shirvane, Sector 1, Nerul, Navi Mumbai 400 706
  Tel. 27721273, 27721274, Email: vivamumbai@vivagroupindia.in
- Jamals Fazal Chambers, 26 Greams Road, Chennai 600 006
  Tel. 28294241, 28290304, Email: vivachennai@vivagroupindia.in
- B-103, Jindal Towers, 21/1A/3 Darga Road, Kolkata 700 017
  Tel. 22816713, Email: vivakolkata@vivagroupindia.in
- 7, GF, Sovereign Park Aptts., 56-58, K. R. Road, Basavanagudi, Bengaluru 560 004 Tel. 26607409, Email: vivabangalore@vivagroupindia.in
- 101-102, Moghal Marc Apartments, 3-4-637 to 641, Narayanguda, Hyderabad 500 029
  Tel. 27564481, Email: vivahyderabad@vivagroupindia.in
- First Floor, Beevi Towers, SRM Road, Kaloor, Kochi 682 018
  Tel. 0484-2403055, 2403056, Email: vivakochi@vivagroupindia.in
- 232, GNB Road, Beside UCO Bank, Silpukhuri, Guwahati 781 003
  Tel. 0361-2666386, Email: vivaguwahati@vivagroupindia.in

www.vivagroupindia.com

ISBN: 978-81-309-2285-0

Published by Viva Books Private Limited, 4737/23 Ansari Road, Daryaganj, New Delhi 110 002.

Printed and bound in India.

M0000/M0450

Dedicated
in respectful homage
to
the memory of
Late NJ Yasaswy, founder ICFAI
who was a great institution builder, a legend and a doyen of higher education movement in India and who had sown the seeds of intellectual pursuits in me

It is generally acknowledged that the national competitive capabilities and innovative capacity can be significantly improved by investment in the human resource development sector, especially at the higher education level. However, the present pattern of investment in higher education requires a drastic redirection to enable our stock of human resource to cope with the challenges of the global competitive environment.

– M. Anandakrishnan
Chairman,
Board of Governors, IIT, Kanpur
(from 'Convergence and Integration of Knowledge System: Current Compulsions)

Contents

Foreword

Engineering Education is the preferred choice of a majority of Indian school- leavers, mainly because of the perceived employment potential, in comparison to other alternatives. The so called "circuit branches", viz. CSE, IT, ECE, have been the most popular in recent years because of the phenomenal growth of the IT and ITeS sectors.

Our Engineering Education system is perhaps the largest in the world, comprising 3393 engineering colleges with an admission capacity of 1.485,894 million (according to the 2011–12 AICTE Approval Handbook). Our Engineering Education system is characterized by a plethora of asymmetries or disparities, as evidenced by the regional imbalances, disciplines, location (rural vs urban), employment-seeking vs employment-generating, level (UG vs PG), funding and governance (public vs private), affiliated vs autonomous, etc. The current buzzwords in Higher Education in our country are: access, equity, affordability, inclusion, quality, excellence, etc.

There are several issues of concern with our Engineering Education system. There is a small number of quality institutions dispersed within a large population of mediocre institutions. The faculty shortage at different levels is staggering, unable to cope with accelerating growth in the number of institutions; severe shortage of Ph.D.s particularly in Engineering; and a general reluctance among bright graduates and postgraduates to take up the teaching profession as a career option. The employability of the graduates seems to leave a lot to be desired, with the curricular offerings not matching the employer needs and requirements. While it is demonstrated by the annual WCU rankings that Research is an important dimension of Higher and Professional education, our research involvement and performance are woefully inadequate.

There are, however, continuing efforts to address and tackle these challenges. Institutions are becoming aware of this need to incorporate quality as one of the key action areas, and Ph.D enrolments are on the rise, and faculty emoluments have been considerably enhanced. The TEQIP program of MHRD, supported by the World Bank, are beginning to show results. Technology is being tapped to enhance student learning as well as faculty teaching through NPTEL, NMEICT and National Knowledge Network. A major skill development initiative is being undertaken through the Skill Development Mission. Innovation, being the essential ingredient for global competitiveness, is getting its due share of attention: GoI has declared the coming decade as the *Decade of Innovation*. There are several Higher Education Bills waiting to be passed by the two Houses of Parliament.

It is thus seen that these are exciting times for Engineering Education in the country. There are several prisms or lenses through which this dynamic system may be viewed. Dr. VRK Prasad provides in this book the HRM perspectives of Engineering Education in India, which aspect has received scant attention to date. Dr. Prasad has the requisite background (with his recent Ph.D. work on *The* Business *of HR in Business Schools*) and his recent book entitled "*Education Sector: HR Perspectives*-Vols I & II), to examine Engineering Education from the HR perspective.

He discusses several issues pertaining to Engineering Education in India in Part I, and focuses on HRM Perspectives in Part II. His approach is direct and insightful, and I am sure that this Book will be a valuable resource for all stakeholders of Engineering Education.

Prof R Natarajan
Former Chairman, AICTE &
Former Director, IIT, Madras

Bangalore, May 2012

Preface

Engineering education of late has become the most popular discipline to pursue for the youth of our country, for its sheer employment potential. With the liberalization of the economy, the Indian industry with increasing encouragement from the successive governments is poised for a major growth even to dislodge certain well established economies from their coveted positions. The argument that we are living in a knowledge driven era needs no debate, thus creating, disseminating, acquiring and using knowledge is going to be a significant feature rather an essential requirement of our growth profile. Having passed from industrial to knowledge economy, there is a need to look towards innovation economy to achieve and retain a competitive edge where effective use of the skills of the people would be the need of the hour. National development would take place only when there is lot of emphasis on science and technology and it is gratifying to note that our strides in this area are in the right direction. "If science and technology are to contribute towards national development, then special talents must be developed in the people. The most important investment any country can make, whatever its stage of economic development is in its human resources – in the education and training of its people" (R Natarajan).

Almost three decades in the army followed by yet another one plus in academics made me develop a keen interest in people dimension of the organizations. Human resources in our country have been attracting the attention of rest of the world as value adders and as performance enhancers of the organizations. HR is no longer a compliance player but an active committed participant in the business process that binds people to a course of action relevant to the objective. Sadly there is not much literature on sector specific HRM. Fundamental issues remaining same, subtle differences could exist between a service industry and a manufacturing outfit. The General Agreement on Trade in Services (GATS) included 'education' as a service.

Having forayed into academics in the year 2000 through a well known business school, leading to raising an exclusive HR school, I started noticing a glaring gap between preaching and practicing of HRM. There virtually was nothing like a proper or well organized HRM function as such. The scene was no different elsewhere in the country too, which ultimately led me to my research desk and five long years of hard work landed a "Ph D" in my lap, from a well known university of the country. Thus a book titled 'The Business of HR in Business Schools' was born out of my doctoral thesis.

It was just by a chance that I came across books titled "Technical Education: Current Status and Future Directions Vol I, II & III by R Natarajan (IUP)" which motivated rather goaded me to undertake this work on engineering colleges in similar lines as I did for business schools. The preponderance of engineering colleges especially in four southern states together with Maharashtra and Uttar Pradesh garnering more than two thirds of the total admission capacity in the country is a well known fact. Given the 'service' nature of these institutions, the needs of the stake holders like students, parents, faculty, industry and of the society I feel must be addressed adequately. Of late the employability of the engineers churned out by the mushrooming engineering colleges all over the country has become debatable with industry stalwarts and entrepreneurs like Narayan Murthy founder of Infosys feeling that not more than 25% are employable. This is a pathetic situation with 4321 engineering colleges (AICTE website) in the country with about 134 colleges having been added in 2012 itself (Rediff.com May 31, 2012)

Surprisingly newly established smaller states seem to be faring better as Jharkhand (17 colleges) and Bihar (18 colleges) with just

35 colleges in all maintain 33% employability rate while states like Andhra Pradesh (721 colleges), Tamil Nadu (550 colleges) and Maharashtra (469 colleges) are pretty low at 13%, 9% and 15% approx respectively. Even NCR Delhi (35 colleges) and Himachal Pradesh (21 colleges) both have high employability rate at 40% approx each while Rajasthan and Punjab (colleges between 100–200) are not far behind with around 20% employability. These figures more or less vindicate the above observations of the founder of Infosys. More worrying is the fact that engineers getting employed in IT products services is pathetically low at 4%, while about 18% are absorbed by IT services. This in a way is indicative of the fact that the training has been rather low on creative and analytical areas.

The reasons for low quality engineers could be summarized as supply overtaking the demand with students lacking in aptitude for engineering education, taking it up just because of its availability for the asking, with the scene getting reversed in terms of shortage of qualified faculty where the demand outstrips the supply. Added to this is the basic fact that 'teaching' as a profession is not considered very lucrative in our country and is the last resort when nothing else is available and the promoters of engineering colleges not paying explicit attention to HR aspects of the faculty and staff while the faculty in state sponsored institutions derive benefits by periodic revisions of their compensation etc through various pay commissions' recommendations approved by AICTE/UGC. With large number of private engineering colleges spread all over the country frustration among their faculty is only a natural manifestation which has a linear effect on their morale, motivation and finally on their teaching which ultimately result in a poor product called 'engineers'.

Education accounts for more than $ 3 billion of the world's economy. With private universities under state legislatures and deemed variety coming up everywhere and education sector assuming a corporate character, every private educational institution has become an 'enterprise' by itself. Research has proved that an educational institution is no different from a corporate entity in expecting effective performance from its employees where the objective is the quality student output in case of the former while the latter aims at commercial gain which is more quantitative in nature. If that is so, then HR function in an educational institution is as important as it is in a corporate entity or in a manufacturing unit for that matter. Unfortunately in our country HR as a function is the most neglected area in most of the educational institutions. Not many institutions can boast of an exclusive HR functionary to look into the HR needs of the staff where attention is paid more by default than by design. My work in similar area for business schools has been well received by the concerned academic fraternity. I thought it would be prudent to extend the benefit to engineering college faculty as well who outnumber the management faculty many times over and hence this humble effort. The aim is to provide a 'one point' reference material to heads of engineering colleges specially private ones of whom we have large in number, and who value use of effective HRM practices and consider faculty as a vibrant and vital part of the organization always committed to its success and growth, more so because they enjoy more functional freedom in implementing the practices discussed and suggested in this book in comparison to these heading the state run institutions.

Dr V R K Prasad

Acknowledgements

This effort would not have seen the light of the day but for the support and guidance of Prof R Natarajan, former Chairman AICTE, and former Director IIT, Madras whose enormous works on engineering education have been of great help and inspiration. My special thanks to him for all that and also for his kind and insightful 'Foreword'. I would like to convey my heartfelt thanks to the Indian Society for Technical Education in general and to Prof R Hariharan in particular for providing me with a vast pool of reference material.

Lots of thanks to my colleagues Arnavaz and Ankur who gave the book its present shape with their untiring efforts on the computer.

My special thanks to the various authors of books and articles, magazine and newspaper editors and others from academic and non academic fields from whose publications I borrowed a lot and who were cited formally and my apologies to those left out inadvertently. Nevertheless I greatly appreciate and value their work.

A lot of credit goes to my wife Durga whose constant support kept me going against odds. Many thanks to her and to my children Sudhama, Swathi and Kartik for their encouragement and belief in me.

Lastly, I am grateful to my parents and the great God Almighty as I owe everything in me to them and also for giving me the strength to undertake and complete this book.

Dr V R K Prasad

Introduction

Staffing is one of the basic functions of any management process, and it is through this vital activity one creates the most valuable asset of the organization in terms of its human resources. Human Resource Management (HRM) is the process of acquiring, training, motivating and retaining the right people in the organization so as to achieve its intended and stated objectives. Rightly Megginson termed human resources as 'the total knowledge, skills, creative abilities, talents and aptitudes of an organization's work force as well as the values, attitudes and beliefs of the individuals involved'. Everything depends upon how effectively these resources are identified in the first place (acquisition), provided with relevant skills (trained and developed) and motivated through adequate compensation and rewarding mechanisms, ensuring their commitment, and finally retained to accomplish the organizational goals. The importance of all the above functions need no further emphasis in any type of organization and an educational institution is no exception.

We all agree that any nation's ability to develop, lies in its people and their capabilities, either in terms of extensive application of technology in the industry or in the increase of agricultural produce. In either of the cases the development is not going to take place by default, but the people must be endowed with special talents and skills to produce more and more – technology and education need to hold hands and move together. An educated person may not be able to deliver anything on his own, unless provided with right technical environment to be productive.

However the latest figures released by MHRD (The Times of India, Hyderabad, August 27, 2012) indicate a very bright picture of the higher education scene of the country where in the GER appears to have dramatically increased from 12.4 to 20.2 percent and 26 million students are reported to be studying in 600 universities and 34000 colleges across India.

In India we have 504 universities or institutions of matching level and close to 26000 colleges belonging to state or central governments or to private bodies. Among them, technical education at degree and diploma levels is imparted in 7272 and 2324 institutions respectively. Despite these large number of higher education establishments, within the country, close to 1 lakh students go abroad every year to pursue higher studies and this number is likely to reach a million strong by 2025–30.

Rapid industrialization of the country placed a heavy demand on technology and consequently on technical education, resulting in its phenomenal growth. Thus the 'engineer' has come to occupy the 'centre stage' in the context of our national development firstly by learning and adopting the technology and then by meeting the societal needs. That the 'faculty' who churns out this engineer should be highly proficient is a fact that calls for no debate. If this is the case, then human resource management in an engineering college or in any educational institution is as important as in any other organizations. HRM as a functional discipline is generally a taken for granted activity in an educational institution with little or no specific attention paid to.

Most school leaving students after their 10+2 find engineering education as a popular choice for further education because of its employability potential. To meet this rising demand one saw an exponential growth in the number of engineering colleges across the length and the breadth of the country and an AICTE source says that there are 3393 colleges today with 14.85 lakh seats almost three times to what they were five/six years ago. It is a sad commentary on our education system that a large percentage of these seats remained vacant during the year 2011–2012 forcing hundreds of colleges to get on to the brink of closing their shutters.

Proliferation of these colleges has raised quality related issues, while some have excelled, others became merely teaching shops having been raised more as business ventures than as social initiatives. By and large engineering education in the country, of late has been raising eye brows and weaning away the prospective students to other greener pastures of higher education. Employability of engineering graduates trained by these vast number of colleges has become a debatable issue.

Experts like R. Natarajan (2005) feel that the most important factor for determining the quality of engineering graduates is the quality of the teaching faculty, who unfortunately is there more by default than by design with no specific preparation or training for teaching or any practical experience. Thus in the cause-effect relationship there is an urgent need to take a close look at the very 'makers' of the engineers in the first place, from HRM angle. Strangely for many people while seeking a career in our country, teaching profession comes as the last resort, and is rarely considered worthy of pursuit. Those who can, do, and, those who cannot, teach says it all. The reasons could be social, cultural or even historic. This has led to a situation where HRM in an educational institution is considered irrelevant under the garb 'take care of yourself'. Added to this is the lackadaisical attitude of the ranking agencies who rarely or never focus on HRM or quality of the faculty. One generally saw the same institutes or colleges cornering the top places, year after year, indicating a strange scenario 'best remained best, while the rest continued to slog'. No comprehensive study seems to have been made to identify the real causes behind the present state of poor quality of engineering education in the country and this book is a humble effort in that direction.

The book is divided into two parts. Part I has four chapters. Chapter 1 provides an overview of origin and growth of engineering education in general with special reference to its present status in India. In Chapter 2 the role of technical education in national development is discussed while quality issues in engineering education have been addressed in Chapter 3. Chapter 4 briefly touches upon the existing literature in the area.

Part II consisting of five chapters is fully devoted to various HRM practices like, acquisition (recruitment and selection) skill development (training), knowledge creation (research) performances management, compensation, organizational culture (morale and motivation), retention and leadership/governance etc, each area covered in great details under a separate chapter, or a sub chapter. Most of the HR issues have been grouped under 'motivation & morale' chapter.

The aim is to help the engineering college fraternity in improving their lot and in the process improve the state and the quality of engineering education in the country where every graduate should be employable not only in India but anywhere in the world. Errors and omissions are unintended and suggestions are welcome. The book very briefly touches upon the HRM issues of non teaching staff under the assumption that they would be taken care of, by the institutional /HR heads in the same lines as they do for the faculty. Needless to say that views expressed in the book are purely personal and methods discussed are only suggestive in nature.

Abbreviations

ABET	Accreditation Board for Engineering and Technology
Acad	Academic
Accts	Accounts
Admin	Administration
AICTE	All India Council for Technical Education
AMCAT	Aspiring Minds Computer Adaptive Test
ARWU	American Ranking of World Universities
ASTD	American Society for Training and Development
B.Ed	Bachelor of Education
B.Tech	Bachelor of Technology
BITS	Birla Institute of Technology and Science
CAYT	Career Award for Young Teachers
CBSE	Central Board of Secondary Education
C-DAC	Centre for Developing Advanced Computing
CEUs	Continuous Education Units
CII	Confederation of Indian Industry
Co-ord	Coordinator
CPRHE	Centre for Policy Research in Higher Education
CSE	Computer Sciences Engineering
CSI	Computer Society of India
CSIR	Council of Scientific & Industrial Research
DCE	Delhi College of Engineering
DGM	Deputy General Manager

DTU	Delhi Technological University
DVP	Distinguished Visiting Professorship
E&Y	Ernst & Young
ECE	Electronics/Electrical (as the case may be) and Communication Engineering
ECI	Engineering Council of India
EDC	Entrepreneurship Development Cell
EF	Emeritus Fellowship
Elec	Electrical
ET	Educational Technology
FD	Faculty Development
FDP	Faculty Development Program
FICCI	Federation of Indian Chambers of Commerce and Industry
Fin	Finance
FTP	Faculty Training Program
GATS	General Agreement on Trade in Services
GDP	Gross Domestic Product
GER	Gross Enrolment Ratio
GoI	Government of India
Govt	Government
HOD	Head of the Department
HR	Human Resources
HRD	Human Resource Development
HRM	Human Resource Management
HRP	Human Resource Planning
IBM	International Business Machines
ICFAI	Institute of Chartered Financial Analysts of India
ICT	Information and Communication Technology
ICTACT	ICT Academy of Tamil Nadu
IETE	Institution of Electronics & Telecommunication Engineers

IFEES	International Federation of Engineering Education Societies
IICs	Industry Interface Cells
IIIT	International Institute of Information Technology
IIM	Indian Institute of Management
IIPC	Industry Institute Partnership Cell
IPS	Innovation Promotion Scheme
ISI	Indian Standards Institute
ISTE	Indian Society of Technical Education
IISc	Indian Institute of Science
IIT	Indian Institute of Technology
IIT-B	Indian Institute of Technology-Bombay
INR	Indian Rupee
ISO	International Organization for Standardization
IT	Information Technology
IT-BHU	Institute of Technology, Banaras Hindu University
ITeS	Information Technology Enabled Services
IUP	Icfai University Press
JNTU	Jawaharlal Nehru Technological University
KAP	Knowledge, Application and Personality Development
KBE	Knowledge Based Economy
KIAP	Kanpur Indo American Programme
KMIT	Keshav Memorial Institute of Technology
KPMG	Klynveld Peat Marwick (A Consultancy Firm)
M.Ed	Master of Education
M.Phil	Master of Philosophy
M.Tech	Master of Technology
Mech	Mechanical
MHRD	Ministry of Human Resource Development
MIT	Massachusetts Institute of Technology
MNC	Multi National Company
MODROBS	Modernization and Removal of Obsolescence

MS	Master of Science
NAE	National Academy of Engineering
NAFEN	National Foundation for Indian Engineers
NAFETIC	National Facilities in Engineering & Technology with Industrial Collaboration
NCP	National Co-ordinated Project
NDF	National Doctoral Fellowship
NASSCOM	National Association of Software and Service Companies
NCC	National Cadet Corps
NCERT	National Council of Educational Research and Training
NCR	National Capital Region
NIIT	National Institute of Information Technology
NIT	National Institute of Technology
NKC	National Knowledge Commission
NMEICT	The National Mission on Education Through Information and Communication Technology
NPTEL	National Programme on Technology Enhanced Learning
NSF	National Science Foundation
NTTF	Nettur Technical Training Foundation
NWP	North Western Province
OB	Organisational Behavior
OECD	Organisation for Economic Co-operation and Development
PA	Performance Appraisals
PBAS	Performance Based Appraisal System
PC	Planning and Co-ordination
PG	Post Graduate
PGER	Postgraduate Education and Research
Ph D	Doctor of Philosophy
PISA	Programme for International Students Assessment

PMS	Performance Management System
PR	Public Relations
PRO	Public Relations Officer
PSE	Perceived Self Efficacy
QA	Quality Assurance
QIP	Quality Improvement Program
QS	Quacquarelli Symonds
R&S	Recruitment & Selection
R&C	Research & Consultancy
R&D	Research and Development
RA	Research Associate
REC	Regional Engineering College
RID	Research and Institutional Development
ROI	Return On Investment
RP	Research Park
RPS	Research Promotion Scheme
RTE	Right to Education
SG	Seminar Grant
SPEED	Student Platform for Engineering Education Development
SPSS	Statistical Package for the Social Sciences
SRHE	Society for Research into Higher Education
TA	Teaching Assistant
TEQIP	Technical Education Quality Improvement Program
TG	Travel Grant
TQM	Total Quality Management
TTT	Technical Teacher's Training
UG	Undergraduate
UGC	Universities Grants Commission
UIRCs	University Industry Research Centres
UNESCO	United Nations Educational, Scientific and Cultural Organization

US	United States
USA	United States of America
viz.	that is to say
VP	Visiting Professorship
vs	Versus
WCU	Western Carolina University

PART I

1
The Origin and Growth of Engineering Education in India

"Scientists investigate that which already is; Engineers create that which has never been".

– Albert Einstein

The vital role engineering and technology play in the economic development of a nation both through industrial productivity and agricultural activity needs no further emphasis and India is no exception to this. Knowledge of engineering and technology in India dates back to Indus Valley civilization with well laid out towns, paving way for metallurgy, and skilled craftsmanship in various activities. While the manufacturing activities took place in Kharkhanas, encouraged by the rulers, the technical skills were handed down the generations in the 'Viharas' during Buddist era under 'gurukul' system. These viharas subsequently turned into higher institutions like Nalanda, Vikramshila, Mithila and Takshashila which carved a niche for themselves before getting into oblivion on decline of Buddhism in India.

ORIGIN OF ENGINEERING EDUCATION: BRITISH INDIA

British India saw the first survey school in 1794 in Madras which later got converted to Civil Engineering School in 1857, while in Bengal survey discipline was taught in Mohammedan College (est-1781) and Hindu College (est-1817). Western India was the last entrant in 'survey' teaching with Elphistone Institution in Bombay starting its program in 1844. The first ever college level engineering education was started in Civil Engineering College at Roorkee in 1847, with Lieutnant Maclagan as the Principal, with the active support of James Thomason, then Lieutnant Governor of NWP (North Western Province). This college subsequently was named after its founder in 1854 after the untimely death of Thomason in 1853. This became a role model for other engineering colleges later, opened in Calcutta-(1856), Madras-(1859) and Poona (1864) which later came to be known as Bengal Engineering College (1920), Guindy Engineering College (1920) and Poona College of Engineering (1911) respectively. All these four engineering colleges remained more or less under the control of military engineers till 1930 or so.

Simultaneously the Victoria Jubilee Technical Institute was started in Bombay in 1887 under a private initiative, and yet another one in Ahmedabad got going in 1910 for textile engineering. Teaching of electrical engineering was started for the first time in the country in 1915 by the Indian Institute of Science at Bangalore and Banaras Hindu University took the lead in starting classes in mechanical engineering discipline in 1917. The Indian School of Mines at Dhanbad commenced training in mining and geology in 1926. In the years that followed, the number of engineering colleges registered a small growth to reach a figure of 46 with an intake of 2500 students mainly to cater for governmental needs as very few engineers at that time could be absorbed in the private sector. Later NR Sarkar Committee constituted in the year 1945 recommended establishment of higher technical education institutions on the lines of Massachusetts Institute of Technology (MIT) in the USA, and creation of a national agency called All India Council of Technical Education (AICTE) (1945) to co-ordinate the growth of technical education in the country. However the diploma education that time being imparted through 53 institutions handling about 3620 students in 1947 was the first to be tackled with, by the AICTE, and it was only after independence the second major recommendation of the Sarkar Committee took shape in the establishment of the first

Indian Institute of Technology (IIT) in Kharagpur in 1951 followed by four more in Bombay (1958), Madras (1960), Delhi (1961) and Kanpur (1959) in the next 10 years.

POST INDEPENDENCE SCENARIO

The government, after independence, realized the importance of technical education in the country and constituted number of commissions/committees to go into the state of affairs and recommend measures to improve the standards. The IITs which came into existence on Sarkar Committee recommendations and that of The Radhakrishna Commission (1949) became 'centres of excellence' and continue to remain so till date in producing quality engineers, who win world wide recognition. Planning commission went about in constituting yet another committee called Engineering Personnel Committee (1955) which recommended establishment of a Regional Engineering College (REC) which started at eight, rose to fifteen by 1972 to provide each state with one REC at least. Two more were added later in Jallundhar (1985) and Hamirpur (1989). The Thaker Committee (1959) and Kothari Commission (1964) recommended encouragement of post graduate engineering education by funding at least 100 PhDs annually and stressed the need for practical training and industry institute interface. Around the same time a Technical Teacher's Training (TTT) and QIP (Quality Improvement Program) was also started in various technical institutions to offset the shortage of quality faculty.

Nayudamma Committee constituted twice in the year 1979-80 and again in 1986 went into PG education in engineering & technology, and reviewed the functioning of IITs, and made recommendations with regard to academic flexibility, focus on engineering and mobility of faculty etc, which were implemented. AICTE's Rama Rao Committee (1995-99) recommended the increase in duration of M.Tech course from 18 months to 21 months (which was actually increased to 24 months) enhancement of scholarship amount to PG students, enrolling of foreign students to PG programs, assured placements through active linkages with potential employers and introduction of doctoral programs at national level, etc, among various other measures. In a way this committee's report brought in lot of improvements in the PG level engineering education in the country. Then came in RA Mashelkar Committee (1998) which recommended conversion of RECs into NIsT (National Institutes of Technology) with the status of a deemed to be university and structural changes in their governance which again is a landmark reform as till then, the RECs were academically dependent on the local state run universities, an arrangement which had its own problems. UR Rao Committee (2003) recommended removal of regional inequities in engineering education addressing faculty, shortage issues, and the need for planning and co-ordination in the working of AICTE. P. Rama Rao Committee yet again in 2004 went into increase in intake of IITs, increase in their fund allocation, and raising of new IITs, without compromising on quality etc.

As can be seen from the above the government having realized the critical need for the technical education kept on increasing fund allocation with each successive five year plan resulting in establishing IITs and RECs till the 3rd five year plan, while reducing the allotment during the 4th plan (1969–74) from 25 to 13 percent, finding it difficult to meet the enormous demand for technical education. To tide over this in the mid seventies it was decided to grant permission to private players to start engineering colleges on self-supporting basis. On their part the government constituted Joshi Committee to identify the institutions that could be converted into IIsT as against a more expensive proposition of a starting new ones, and the committee did identify seven such institutions paving way for Anandakrishnan Committee (2006) which actually visited these institutions. While the action on the conversion of these was still on its way, the government announced the establishment of eight new IITs and conversion of IT-BHU into IIT, and by 2010 the said establishment of new ones and conversion of a few more reportedly got completed.

Consequent to the decision to encourage private participation in engineering education, number of engineering colleges came up specially in Andhra (280) Tamil Nadu (268), Maharashtra (171) and Karnataka (128) apart from all other states in the country totaling to 1511 with a total intake of 550986 by the year 2006-2007 though only 4396,689 seats were reported to have been filled up leaving over lakh of seats unfilled even at that time. This phenomenon did not deter the promoters who came up with more and more colleges year after year (see the table 1 below) and at the current academic session (2011–12) the number of colleges are 3393 with a total capacity of 14,85,894 seats of which few lakhs (more than 2 lakhs) reportedly having remained unfilled. This is despite the fact that the entry norms have been relaxed by AICTE by lowering the minimum score to join an engineering college. This does not angur well for a developing economy like India.

Table 1

Year	*Engg Colleges*	*Students*
2006–07	1511	550986
2007–08	1668	653290
2008–09	2388	841018
2009–10	2972	1071896
2010–11	3222	1314594
2011–12	3393	1485894

(Source: AICTE)
(The Times of India, Hyderabad, Oct 31, 2011)

As on 27th Nov 2011 (Deccan Chronicle, Hyderabad) Andhra Pradesh has about 710 engineering colleges with an intake of 3,05066 seats the highest in the country, with almost half of the colleges (312) located in and around twin cities of Hyderabad and Secunderabad alone. The state govt is all set to impose a ban on setting up more engineering colleges unless they are planned either in four backward districts or propose to offer programs in emerging technologies.

Uncontrolled Growth

As can be seen from the table above that there has been a steady rise in the number of engineering colleges from a mere 50 in 1950 to 1511 in 2006–2007. The rise has also been noticed in the average intake per institution which increased from 74 in 1950 to 346 in 2006. Most of the growth came in the preceding ten years (1996–2006) where in the number of colleges grew by 1121 averaging 100 plus per year. Post 2006 the growth has been exponential and phenomenal where in by 2011–2012 the numbers rose from 1511 to 3393 registering a 100 plus percent growth all in a matter of five years, while the seats increased almost three fold from 550986 to 1485894. This is despite the fact that few lakhs of seats across the country remained unfilled, which again did not deter the promoters to come up with more number of engineering colleges even after 2011 (3400 last reported). This uncontrolled growth in quantity is seriously reflecting on the quality of the education being imparted in terms of the affiliating university system, shortage of qualified faculty, grossly inadequate infrastructure, outdated curricula and evaluation systems, lack of academic atmosphere, and business oriented and authoritative governance all of which have converted these institutions of higher technical education into virtual teaching shops.

The most obvious consequence of all the above issues is the unemployable and poor quality of engineering graduates who are neither technically competent nor generally proficient. A survey conducted by Purple Leap covering the states of Delhi NCR, Punjab & Haryana, Madhya Pradesh, Rajasthan, Uttarakhand, UttarPradesh, Karnataka, Tamil Nadu, Andhra Pradesh, Orissa, West Bengal and Maharashtra revealed that among 34000 sample size of final year engineering students across 198 tier 2, 3 and 4 colleges of the country with over 60 percent marks, only 12 percent are employment ready, 52 percent being trainable and a whopping 36 percent not even trainable. Most concern causing issue is the lack of generic and analytical skills considered natural for engineering students. Even in technical skills only 42 percent barely make the grade across the sectors. Fortunately 6 percent which constitute the tier 1 engineering colleges among the total of 3400, are turning out as many readily employable engineering graduates as the rest all put together. (The Hindu, Hyderabad Jul 27, 2012).

Yet another report by Aspiring Minds (www.rediff.com dated Jul 25, 2012) on a survey conducted on 55000 engineering students who graduated in 2011 from 250 plus engineering colleges through AMCAT (Aspiring Minds Computer Adaptive Test) covering areas like vocabulary, grammar, and comprehension brought out the following:

- More than 25% do not possess the comprehending skills to understand engineering curriculum
- Only 57% can write grammatically correct English
- Only 42–45% demonstrate English language capability required of a knowledge based industry
- Only 27% possess business communication skills

While the main reasons for this state of affairs have already been mentioned above, certain other causative factors are

- Poor quality of 10+2 education and wide variation in the standards across the states
- Lack of rigor in imparting the engineering education
- More text book, examination and grade orientation over delivery or acquisition of application related knowledge ("Sadly most young Indian Engineers never have a chance to learn their unwritten skills" – James Trevelyan)
- Lack of academic integrity among students by resorting to malpractices in exams, and dissertation submissions (Ghost writers: Sunday Times of India, Hyderabad, Jun 12, 2012)
- Students taking up engineering courses for reasons other than making a career in that particular field/discipline, like social status, pursue higher studies abroad and enter

into an MNC in IT area or take up management program and seek career in an unrelated area etc

- Students taking admissions in engineering programs merely to earn government scholarships (Andhra Pradesh)and take up other avocations
- Lack of attention by the college management towards developing employability skills among the students
- Lack of orientation towards applicability and practicality in our professional institutions (Shreekanth Sambrani)

The quality of engineering education and consequently that of the graduates produced shall continue to remain a serious issue unless the monitoring/regulatory bodies come down heavily on the governance mechanisms. Silver lining is number of private operators have realized the value of 'quality' and are taking adequate steps to improve upon.

> *Good engineering liberates human effort for social developments such as governance, healthcare, education, social services and even recreation*
>
> – James Trevelyan
> University of Western Australia
> (How to Become an Expert Engineer)

AICTE

Tremendous growth in technical education brought out the need to regulate it by a statutory body AICTE which was initially formed as an advisory body in Nov 1945. The All India Council of Technical Education assumed statutory status by an Act of Parliament in 1987, and is made responsible for proper planning, co-ordination and development of technical education in the country among various other disciplines like management, pharmaceutical, architecture, hotel management educations etc. The AICTE accredits post graduate and graduate programs under specific categories at Indian institutions as per its charter. It is assisted by 10 Statutory Boards of Studies in various disciplines. AICTE has its headquarters in New Delhi with regional offices located at Kolkata, Chennai, Kanpur, Mumbai, Chandigarh, Guwahati, Bhopal, Bangalore, Hyderabad and Gurgaon.

The objectives of the AICTE Act 1987 are reproduced below

OBJECTIVES

The AICTE Act of 1987

AICTE is vested with statutory authority for planning, formulation and maintenance of norms and standards, quality assurance through school accreditation, funding in priority areas, monitoring and evaluation, maintaining parity of certification and awards and ensuring coordinated and integrated development and management of technical education in the country as part of the AICTE Act No. 52 of 1987.

The AICTE Act, stated verbatim reads:

To provide for establishment of an All India Council for Technical Education with a view to the proper planning and co-ordinated development of the technical education system throughout the country, the promotion of qualitative improvement of such education in relation to planned quantitative growth and the regulation and proper maintenance of norms and standards in the technical education system and for matters connected therewith.

Current objective

In order to improve upon the present technical education system, the current objectives is to modify the engineering curriculum as follows

1. Greater emphasis on design oriented teaching, teaching of design methodologies, problem solving approach.
2. Greater exposure to industrial and manufacturing processes.

3. Exclusion of outmoded technologies and inclusion of the new appropriate and emerging technologies.
4. Greater input of management education and professional communication skills.

AICTE Bureaus

The AICTE comprises nine bureaus, namely:

- Faculty Development (FD) Bureau
- Undergraduate Education (UG) Bureau
- Postgraduate Education and Research (PGER) Bureau
- Quality Assurance (QA) Bureau
- Planning and Co-ordination (PC) Bureau
- Research and Institutional Development (RID) Bureau
- Administration (Admin) Bureau
- Finance (Fin) Bureau
- Academic (Acad) Bureau

For each bureau, adviser is the bureau head who is assisted by technical officers and other supporting staff. The multidiscipline technical officer and staff of the Council are on deputation or on contract from government departments, University Grants Commission, academic institutions, etc.

Source:http://en.wikipedia.org/wiki/All_India_Council_for_Technical_Education

Though a couple of years ago, as a part of reforms in education sector, AICTE and UGC were reportedly planned to be closed down in favour of larger and stronger regulatory bodies, in their place but the same is yet to take shape, on the ground.

2

Role of Technical Education in National Development

'Our progress as a nation can be no swifter than our progress in education. The human mind is our fundamental resource'

– John F Kennedy

There is no denial of the fact that our country has achieved great success in the areas of Science and Technology notably in the strategic sectors like Space, Nuclear Power and Information Technologies. A large percentage of the credit for the strides the country has made goes to our technical education system, which is one of the biggest in the world today. Despite a continuous spate of recessions, Indian economy has been registering a fair and steady growth and is tipped to become a force to reckon with in the not so distant future. Education is the back bone of any society, and higher education in general and technical educations in particular have a vital role to play in the present day knowledge driven era. The industrial development of the country propelled the need for technical manpower which by itself became the major aim in opening vast number of engineering colleges in the country leading to national development.

A nation consists of people who become its human resource and their development through education and technology assumes critical significance. They in turn harness the natural resources to increase the agricultural and industrial production to foster economic growth for the country. In this process technical education or engineering education has a pivotal role to play, as it leads the country to move from under developed to developing and finally to join the league of developed nations. Technology by itself is a critical element which both can be developed indigenously and imported based not only on cost considerations but also on its applicability, suitability, and utility in the native country. To that extent an engineer must not only become a promoter of technology, but its creator too, to address the problems faced by the society which could be all encompassing. With the technology changing at break neck speed, there is a strong need to adopt the change and move on. Engineers must also envisage the problems likely to be confronted by the society on a proactive basis rather to address them reactively. To that extent the engineering education apart from imparting the relevant technical knowledge to the student must instill the senses of inquisitiveness and of responsibility, ability to work through unclear situations all with the idea of national or societal development in the hindsight. The developments in science and technology would have little or no relevance if skilled manpower in terms of engineers is not available to apply the same for the benefit of the human life. So much so in the present day, knowledge driven economics of the world, engineering education has become a survival tool both at individual and also at society levels (MS Ananth). KAP (knowledge application and personality development – VRK Prasad) skills today have assumed greater significance than ever before. Knowledge provides an individual with sufficient insights into the functional area or discipline, while the application or the know-how is the ability to put the knowledge so gained to a productive use. The last but the most important of all the three attributes is the 'personality development' or the 'character building' through which a young adolescent person is transformed into a mature adult ready to render service to the society. By and large engineering colleges across the country with their huge numbers have been reportedly concentrating only on the first aspect of imparting curriculum related knowledge, thus highlighting the strong need to address the other two aspects too, which are as important.

> *'The role of the curriculum is not simply to impart knowledge but also to influence students' attitudes, and a key element in an engineering curriculum must be the development in students of the attitude of mind required to handle typical engineering problems'*
>
> – R Natarajan

In a developing economy, the curriculum of engineering education being highly professional in nature has a vital role to play in providing the aspirants with a broad based knowledge and training, so that they could become effective in nation building process.

While there is no debate on the importance of technical education in national development, some experts (Vijay K Thadani and Parimal Mandke) have propounded that the emerging knowledge economy is forcing us to shift from task centricity to process centricity across industries and sectors where they opine, that education sector is no exception. Process-centric activities involve a set of inter-related and inter connected sub activities and people handling them forming a continuum where each performer is of equal importance unlike the task-centric process which is wholly controlled by the top few only.

To derive maximum benefit out of this process centric approach, education needs a total review, in terms of content, delivery, and evaluations etc, while the existing system is filled with far too much theoretical rigidity with little or no orientation towards industry needs. There is also a strong need to address the learning requirements of working professionals both within and outside the formal systems. NIIT (National Institute of Information Technology) is reported to have successfully developed a model for post secondary technical education outside the formal system to meet the requirements of both the aspirants and the industry with their innovatively designed programs.

Yet another issue is of over emphasis in teaching and examinations making the whole process a teacher centric one

(Pedagogy). If the student has to serve the society and excel in his progression then the emphasis should be as much on learning per se, by the student adopting a student centric approach (Androgogy) M. Adithan and Ing. BVA Rao suggest a shift from 'Instructional Paradigm to Learning Paradigm' in the engineering curriculum by suggesting certain additional courses such as

- System concept and modeling
- Critical thinking and problem solving
- Project planning and management
- Creativity and innovation
- Entrepreneurship and Small Business Development
- Knowledge Management
- Science & Technology development to meet societal needs
- Economics, civics, sociology and human biology.

On close scrutiny we can observe that, all the above aspects constitute a major part of the national development process as such; yet another suggestion to intensify the role of engineering education in national development comes in the form of 'Panchsheel' of Technical Education in the 21st century (PB Sharma) as

- Troika of education, research and innovations imbibing scientific values and professional morality
- World class curriculum design and delivery, world class knowledge infrastructure
- Seamless integration of science and engineering
- Research driven, industry relevant innovations
- Network with select world class universities.

Putting all the above to a good use the erstwhile DCE (Delhi College of Engineering) and now DTU (Delhi Technological University) is reported to have developed, the DCE Hybrid Car, the DCE Unmanned Aerial Vehicle, the DCE Robotic Submarine, the DCE Super Mileage Vehicle, the DCE Solar Car, the DCE Intelligent Ground Vehicle, and the DCE Moon Buggy which are a tribute to the innovative skills of the young students and the guiding spirit of the dedicated faculty. This proves that 'Heutogogy' as "...... a desire to go beyond the simple acquisition of skills and knowledge as a learning experience (Hase & Kenyon 1990) is as important as pedagogy and androgogy in the learning process.

INSTITUTES OF EXCELLENCE

There is little or no doubt in acknowledging the fact that the central government's initiatives through IITs, NITs and IIITs, IISc, and ISI etc have been playing a major role in the development of the human resources (technical manpower) of the country. In fact India is rightly proud of their international standing (IK Bhat) but their numbers are not adequate for the size of a country like ours while planning to produce global engineers. Government on its part is doing its best in taking the quality engineering education to the door step of the rural youth through IIITs (Eg: Andhra Pradesh) and upgrading some good engineering colleges to IIT status. The aim in establishing these centres of excellence (specially IITs) was to produce world class engineers but somewhere down the line this objective seems to have got diluted with students running more after the 'brand' than they do for quality engineering education. The coaching system is helping in cracking the entry barriers of these elite institutions, which produce engineers who venture into other areas like management and software etc (RK Tadepalli). Though it is a human resources developmental gain for IT industry and other corporates but is a major loss for the actual engineering industry as a whole. The problem starts at the grass roots level where the young aspirant appears for the entrance examination with the ultimate aim of taking up management program with a top business school and land a well paid corporate job. The acquisition of engineering knowledge during the course gets merely limited to making the grades in the examinations and not to apply the same later in actual working life since he knows for sure that he won't have to. Thus there is a little disconnect between the objectives set forth and the actual achievements in these institutions, though quality student output is remarkable in its own way, as many of the alumni have made it to the top echelons not only at home but abroad too (Raghuram G Rajan, noted economist).

The IITs have a chequered origin dating back to pre independence era (1946) of 22 members Nalini Ranjan Sarkar Committee who recommended establishment of technical institutions on the lines of MIT in the US. Consequently the institutions came up in Kharagpur (1950–51 with the help of MIT), Bombay (1957- supported by UNESCO and USSR), Kanpur (1959 benefited from KIAP – Kanpur Indo American Programme forming a consortium of nine American Universities), Madras (1961 through Indo German Agreement – Bonn), and Delhi (1963- in collaboration with Imperial College, London) – The IITs at Guwahati and Roorkee are the late entrees to the scene in 1995 and 2001. Eight more IITs have been established in Bhubaneshwar, Gandhinagar, Hyderabad, Indore, Jodhpur, Kanpur, Patna and Ropar to cater to the weaker sections of the society (V. Sethuraman). Though the above institutions have been delivering more than their bit in producing world class manpower (may not be 'engineers') but the down side is none of them figure even in top 200 places of rankings of Shanghai (ARWU – The American Ranking of World Universities) compiled by Shanghai Jiao Tong University), QS (Quacquarelli Symonds) World University Rankings, and the Times Higher Education World University Rankings etc. It is of little consolation that few of our IITs and Universities do figure once in a while at low levels in these rankings. Ironically engineering graduates produced by these elite institutes either cross the shores or seek careers in different areas.

Next in the list, come the National Institutes of Technology (NITs) about of 20 of them (erstwhile Regional Engineering Colleges – RECs) which enjoy the autonomy as IITs with the status of 'deemed to be universities'. Number of private players like BITS (Pilani, Goa and Hyderabad) and BITS Mesra Ranchi, TIFR, Thapar Institute of Engineering and Technology, Patiala etc have contributed in their own way in bringing out quality engineers from their campuses, and have become institutes of excellence.

With such large number of quality institutions sponsored by the state and a matching response from the private sector, and number of reforms in the pipe line the future of the technical education in our country looks quite bright.

> *'India has a good education system, but this can be better. Earlier Europeans dominated the scene. But the situation is rapidly changing and now Asian countries especially India, are producing great talents. This is mainly due to good education and a democratic process that provide the right kind of environment for one to go creative*
>
> – Tobias Degsel
> The Educator, Nobel Museum of Stockholm

NEED OF GLOBAL PERSPECTIVE FOR AN ENGINEER

All other factors being equal, no national developmental process can be considered complete unless the international community or rest of the world truly recognizes a country as 'developed' in the real sense of the word; Globalization today has become a ground reality where knowledge, ideas, cultures, resources and people move across the countries. Internationalization of technical education in terms of suitable curriculum, teaching methodologies, learning modes, research, student/faculty exchange, and institutional agreements etc is an inescapable aspect of globalization (UNESCO Education Position Paper on 'Higher Education in a Globalised Society', UNESCO 2004). Though focusing on one, students need to develop a multi discipline approach to create innovative products and services. Information and Communication Technology (ICT) tools have been of great help in this regard. Teaching methods may shift to being student centric in preference to the conventional teacher-centric one, by teacher donning the role of a facilitator. This will encourage the students to resort to self learning on their own, also from their peers, and even from the environment, as espoused in our Vedas *(Acharyat Padamadatte, Padam Sishya Swamedhaya,Padam*

Sahabrahmacharibhyaha, Sesham Kalakramenacha – meaning 'teacher imparts only one fourth of the knowledge, student learns one fourth on his own, yet another quarter of knowledge comes from his peers, the remaining knowledge student acquires from the environment as the time passes'). Engineers are also required to be cautious of environmental degradation, and work with only sustainable technologies. *("God has given us enough for our needs, not for our greed" – Mahatma Gandhi)*

The US National Academy of Engineering (NAE) in a study titled 'The Engineers of 2020: Visions of New Century" (Published by the National Academic Press) outlined the working domain of the future engineers as they say "The engineer of 2020 will be faced with myriad challenges, creating aggressive and defensive solutions at the macro, and micro scales in preparation for positive dramatic changes in the world. Engineers will be expected to anticipate and prepare for potential catastrophes such as biological terrorism; water and food contamination; infrastructure damage to roads, bridges, buildings, and the electricity grid; and communication breakdown in the internet, telephony, radio and television. Engineers will be asked to create solutions that minimize the risk of complete failure and at the same time prepare backdrop solutions that enable rapid recovery, reconstruction and deployment. In short they will face problems qualitatively similar to those they already face today"

Technology is going to form part of every day life what with more than 60% of Indian population having access to mobile telephony, automobile revolution leaving no space for the humans on the roads and air travel once considered a luxury reaching the door step of the average Indian. Indian IT professionals making a mark for themselves in the Silicon Valley, while doing the country proud at home, with millions employed in IT, ITeS, and allied industries, the country is poised for taking a big technological leap and the 7.4 lakh engineers the country produces every year have a vital role to play in this gamut of activities.

ENGINEER OF 2020

While NAE study identified certain attributes required of an 'Engineer of 2020; Continental AG through yet another study involving eight worldwide universities well known for their engineering programs focuses on similar traits for a Global Engineer as listed in the table below

Table 1. Attributes and Traits of a Global Engineer 2020

NAE	*Continental AG*
• Strong Analytical Skills	• Technically Adept
• Practical Ingenuity	• Broadly knowledgeable
• Creativity	• Commercially Savvy
• Basic business management Principles	• Multilingual
• Leadership	• Culturally aware
• High Ethical standards and strong sense of professionalism	• Knowledge about world markets
• Dynamism, resilience agility and flexibility	• Professionally flexible and mobile
• Lifelong learning Attitude	

(Source: Profile of Engineering Education in India: Status, Concerns and Recommendations www.inae.org/book/profilebook.pdf)

Yet another concept of the 'World Class Engineer' was reported to have been developed at the Penn State University in co-operation with the Leonhard Center Advisory Board (R Natarajan 2005) consisting of the following six dimensions

- Awareness of the world
- Solid Foundation and Grounding in a selected engineering discipline
- Technical breadth and multi disciplinary knowledge
- Effectiveness in Team work and Group operations
- Versatile and Innovative
- Customer oriented

As we consolidate our position as a **Knowledge Society** more by creating additional knowledge than by using the existing one, engineering education plays a dominant role in shaping the destiny of the country in its march towards an 'Innovation Society'. India with its demographic advantage is at the threshold of making its beginning while the rest of the world watches it with bated breath.

> *If we are to make progress we must not repeat history but make a new one*
>
> – Mahatma Gandhi

3

Challenges and Quality Issues in Engineering Education

"This is the most exciting period in human history for science and engineering. The explosive advances in knowledge, instrumentation, communication and computational capabilities create a mind-boggling playing field for the next Generation.......... As we think about the plethora of challenges, it is important in my view, to remember that students are driven by passion, curiosity, engagement and dreams..... Despite our best efforts to plan their education, to a large extent we simply help them to wind them up, and then step back to watch the amazing results

– Charles Vest, President MIT, Jul 2004

CHALLENGES

We are talking of close to a million and a half of intake of engineering aspirants at the close of 2011–12 admission seasons in our country and that's a sizeable number by any standards. Yet the demand for engineering education does not appear to be on the wane, especially for those institutions offering quality education both in the public and the private sectors. As the economy hinges around noticeable rise despite the recessionary trends elsewhere in the world the demand for engineering personnel in India in IT, infrastructure, manufacturing and service sectors has been growing exponentially.

An estimate says that India will have nearly 2.5 million jobs in IT and ITeS sectors alone in the year 2012.

If we want to join the company of 'developed' nations through a double digit growth there is an urgent need to boost the present GER (Gross Enrolment Ratio) from the present 15% to say 30% in the next 10 years which means further increase in the rate of growth of engineering education. We at 3.5 science and technology personnel per 1000 population are lagging far behind countries like USA (55) and China (88), and even smaller ones like South Korea (45.9), Germany (76), Israel (76) and Japan (110). Yet another issue is the cost factor being on the higher side weighs heavily against the poorer sections of the society. Girls do not show much interest in pursuing engineering education though the situation has improved reasonably well with the rising employment opportunities in IT and ITES sectors. Reforms in terms of caste/ class/category based reservations, fee waivers/ concessions, scholarships by governments both at centre and state level have improved the situation to a considerable extent. Then there is an uneven distribution of engineering colleges across the country with more than 60% of them concentrated in the Southern, South Western and the Western parts. The north eastern region consisting of eight small states is the most neglected, even for the under graduate engineering education with virtually no facilities for PG level. Despite some private sector players opening up institutions in these areas this regional imbalance and disparity is hindering the development at national level. While the private sector looks at the ROI (Return on investment) it is the government which needs to address this localized sensitive issue, and it is a challenge by itself. Yet another challenge being faced the regulatory body is the preponderance of engineering colleges in the suburbs of the urban areas making it difficult for the rural youth to reach them unless they shift to cities at a heavy cost to their parents. This has further aggravated the existing imbalance situation and the states need to encourage private players with incentives to open up colleges in rural or else still better would be to grant further permissions for opening new colleges in rural areas only henceforth, with saturation point having already been reached in urban and even in semi urban areas.

State is doing its best in opening up more IITs and IIITs and such like institutions but the increasing numbers are not able to match up to quality requirements mainly because of lack of adequate resources in terms of finances, infrastructure and quality faculty. Added to this is the rigid outlook of the university systems whose reforms in various qualitative aspects get struck or embroiled in bureaucratic hassles. Then there is little regard for the industry needs, and their inability to put the fresh graduates to productive use straightaway without formally training them at a considerable expense. External interference from politicians, students and employee unions cause further erosion in the quality of students being churned out. Leaving top few, no extensive use of technology is being made in most of the engineering colleges across the country where conventional mode of academic delivery still rules the roost. Despite the advances made in the IT area, by the country ET (Educational Technology) is yet to make its mark in the class rooms of the engineering colleges. The internet is being used by the youth more for their personal recreation than for pursuing any academic interests. There is limited or nil practical industry exposure facility to engineering students due to paucity of industries in the vicinity of the colleges as a result the projects undertaken by the students would mostly be academic in nature or mere reproduction of the reports prepared by their seniors. Shortage of qualified faculty is one of the most serious challenges being faced by the engineering colleges - yet another challenge typical to our country is the perception of some parents in viewing engineering education as a social opportunity in the matrimonial market while it is perceived as a business opportunity by few others.

There is little or no research orientation in the teaching as one hardly finds an engineering graduate taking up research within the country unless he goes abroad to pursue MS-Ph D combination, with the result back home there is an acute shortage of Ph D qualified faculty. In a typical affiliation system, colleges enjoy no academic freedom in frequently revising their curricula to suit industry needs. Pursuance of a particular discipline or branch by students is getting more market driven than aptitude oriented which results in high admissions and output in one particular area at the expense of others. While the UG colleges have had a mushrooming growth, the PG level facilities continue to remain scanty. Finally the over emphasis on quantity over quality has by itself become a challenge which needs to be addressed on 'most urgent' basis if engineering education has to really form part of the national developmental process.

QUALITY ISSUES

> *"I am very big believer in equal opportunity as opposed to equal outcome. Equal opportunity to me more than anything, means a great education. May be even more important than a great family life. We could make sure that every young child in this county got a great education. We fall for short of that. I know from our education that if I had not encountered two or three individuals that spent extra time with me I am sure I would have been in jail"*
>
> – Steve Jobs

The unprecedented growth in engineering education in the last few years resulted in deterioration of the quality of the engineering graduates. The growth has been more in the private sector, mostly under the university affiliation system which by itself suffered in terms of outdated curriculum, evaluation systems, and typical bureaucratic hurdles. Added to this is the poor quality of infrastructure, shortage of qualified faculty leading to still poorer teaching and learning processes and lack of innovative and proactive measures in imparting quality education that have led to a situation where only 25–30% of engineering graduates are reported to be employable (Nasscom – Mckinsey Report- 2005) in IT/ITES sectors. This is forcing the industry to even absorb the low quality graduates and train them to be productive at a very heavy cost. However the basic issue remains that 'only a quality teacher produces a quality student'. Even a quality teacher needs a right academic ambience in terms of laboratories and library resources and state of the art teaching aids to impart quality education. Understandably the Govt having realized the importance of quality teaching is embarking upon a large training of engineering faculty through 10th–12th five year plans, and encouraging engineering graduates to take up post graduate courses to enter into teaching profession. Now does a doctorate in any discipline form a surety for teaching ability? Can a Ph D holder really articulate upon and impart knowledge that he had created during his research period, or can he further create more knowledge, nurture talent, and light fire of inquisitiveness in the bellies of the students? are some of the pertinent questions one needs to raise. 'Quality' despite all its high sounding definitions given by various theorists simply means "student's satisfaction in learning what he did and his capability to apply it", which more or less summarizes the Barnett's classification of perception of quality in higher education in terms of *objectivist, relativist and development* etc. The National Science Foundation (NSF) Task Force on TQM in Engineering Education (1994) has come out with the following statement on quality of engineering education.

"Quality Engineering Education is the development of intellectual skills and knowledge that will equip graduates to contribute to society through productive and satisfying engineering careers, as innovators, decision makers and leaders in the global economy of the 21st century.

Quality Engineering Education demands a process of continuous improvement of and dramatic innovation in student, employer and societal satisfaction by systematically and collectively evaluating and refining the system, practices and culture of Engineering Education Institutions".

Quality is not one man's show, in fact it is a combination of factors at management, faculty, institutional head and finally at students' level, where all the four constituents have to play their roles to the best of their abilities as outlined in the 'quality policy' of the institution. How does the quality in engineering colleges come about when Indian students rank second last in global test among 73 countries that participated in the two hour test for a half a million students for reading, maths and science in the Programme for International Students Assessment (PISA) conducted annually to evaluate education system world wide by the OECD (Organisation for Economic Co-operation and Development) Secretariat.

Surprisingly China's Shanghai province scored the highest in all the three parameters. This state of affairs is all the more alarming as two developed states Tamil Nadu and Himachal Pradesh who traditionally rank high on human development parameters and considered as more progressive states, have been picked up for the study, where other states could have been much worse off.

Despite this, a ray of hope flickers in the form of private participation in higher education which accounts for about four-fifths of enrolment in professional higher education and one third in overall higher education. According to FICCI-E&Y analysis (Mint, Hyd, Dec 20, 2011) to achieve the 30% target GER by 2020 as desired by the government about 25 million additional seats need to be created over the next eight years with an overall investment of INR 1 million crore at INR 0.4 million average investment per seat. This calls for a huge investment by the private players assuming their present share continues. FICCI- Synovate study – further emphasizes the fact that private operators offer value for money in comparison to government run institutions in terms of quality education and placements. Private players have been largely responsible to increase GERs substantially in countries like USA (1999–71%, 2008–83%) Japan (from 45 to 58%), and Malaysia (from 23% to 32%) as they offer the vital ingredients of a sound education system in terms of access, equity and quality.

Accreditation is a method of assuring the beneficiaries or the stakeholders on the quality aspects of education imparted by the institutions. The National Knowledge Commission (NKC) had suggested licencing of a large number of private organizations to undertake accreditation responsibility. Accordingly the Central Government has formulated a draft legislative proposal namely "National Accreditation Regulatory Authority for Higher Educational Institutions Bill 2009" for the creation of a National Authority for regulating Accreditation of all higher educational institutions in the country (M. Ananda Krishnan). Pending that we have the NBA (National Board of Accreditation) under AICTE laying down the norms and standards while in the US it is undertaken by ABET (Accreditation Board for Engineering and Technology). The Washington Accord (1989) is an agreement between the bodies responsible for accrediting professional engineering degree programs in each of the signatory countries and NBA was granted only provisional membership of this accord in 2007. It is gratifying to note that SRM University (a deemed to be university) at Kattankulathur campus Tamil Nadu received ABET accreditation in 2009 for its B Tech (Electronics and Communication Engineering) Program while more than 50 percent of the technical programs offered in the country are yet to be accredited by NBA as of 2008.

Quality has a direct bearing on the employability of the engineering graduates produced in the institutions. Most of the corporate/companies do find it difficult to make these graduates productive from day one unless they spend considerable time and money in training them even in certain basic areas. This is due to poor industry academia linkage and more of laid down syllabus completion by the colleges with the eye on examinations rather than meeting the requirements of the industry. Yet another issue is of poor or total lack of generation of knowledge through research and innovation where again gap between expectation by the industry and meeting of the same by the academia widens. Soft skills and real time problem solving skills are a big handicap with the present generation of engineering graduates barring those coming out of top few. Quality faculty is a major issue as very few of them engage themselves in active research or publications. It is reported that NIT professors publish less than one paper per year while for IITs it hovers around 1.5 to 2 when the international universities have their faculty publishing at least 4 to 5 papers every year. (NR Shetty-2010). Unless one upgrades his knowledge on a regular basis, he would continue teaching the same material year after year. Students do not find it exciting to attend such classes. More over in some private colleges, some pathetically qualified and lowly paid teachers are taken who indulge more in some lip service than to undertake any quality teaching. Most of the engineering colleges (85%) in the country fall under the 'affiliated to the local state university' category. These affiliated colleges do not have academic or operational autonomy as everything is decided by the university to which they are affiliated. This system curbs their initiative and innovation. Added to this is their over dependence on their parent trust or society for financial matters as the promoter maintains a tight grip on funds.

This is a kind of sandwich or between devil and the deep sea situation and most of them reconcile and resign to their fates putting away all developmental or quality related aspects in the institution. Unlike the business school faculty, engineering colleges faculty tend to shy away from the industry with the result the students are left on their own to either manage projects or somehow produce the reports both of which do not augur well for the quality of the education. Quality faculty cannot be attracted by offering them 'peanuts'. A market driven/AICTE/UGC scale of pay coupled with career growth opportunities, research facilities and other perks and facilities like residential accommodation etc will ensure the stay of quality faculty on the campus.

The international organization for standardization (ISO) defines quality as the 'totality of characteristics of an entity that bears on its ability to satisfy stated and implied needs'. This definition apart, quality as a concept has been baffling human mind. It has become relative to the extent of lying in the eyes of the beholder like the proverbial beauty. Quality and 'beauty' are more difficult to define as to what they really are rather than what they are not. A cliché 'quality is a long and never ending journey and not a destination' is a more appropriate definition which implies the scope for continuous improvement (CI-Kaizen)

Connected with quality are the academic standards of education which constitute a method of ascertaining the level of achievement that a student is expected to reach to gain an academic award of a degree or a diploma. Academic quality is the quantum of learning opportunities provided to the student to achieve this award. These opportunities are in the form of effective teaching, administrative support and proper assessment etc. Now coming on to 'quality education', students go through the learning process to attain the objectives they set for themselves. Quality education is what makes this learning process a joy, by building attractive features into it. Quality forms the core of delivery of these features. Any student will have some learning objectives in the form of seeking knowledge, acquiring skills, an ability to differentiate and finally developing own character so as to become a useful member of the society. Quality education is the one which guarantees to a student, fulfillment of all the four above mentioned objectives.

R. Natarajan in his treatise 'Technical Education: Current Status and Future Directions Vol I (Icfai Books 2005) gives an exhaustive list of factors that promote quality and excellence in engineering colleges at various levels, which are summarized below

- **Head of the Institution:** Initiative, competence, commitment and proper leadership
- **Faculty:** Well qualified with Ph Ds if possible, possess good communication skills, innate desire to teach and excel, passion for life long learning, involve in industry interact, research oriented, active member of professional bodies, inherent desire to produce good citizens for the country

- **Student:** Discipline, motivation to learn, possess strong academic orientation, develop application skills and active participation in extra curricular activities to develop overall personality, and strong communication skills
- **Management:** Needs to look into all HRM aspects of both teaching and non teaching staff and provide adequate infrastructure related facilities to staff and students so that both the groups achieve the objectives they had set for themselves

The learned author also provides lists of indicators of students, faculty and overall quality of engineering education as shown in the table below

Table 1. Indicators of Student, Faculty and Overall Quality

Indicators of Student Quality	*Indicators of Faculty Quality*	*Indicators of Overall Quality*
Qualifications and diversity of entering students	Recruitment and retention success; diversity	The use of strategic planning processes
Rate of retention to graduation	Amount of non-academic engineering experience	External engagement: K-12, industry, community, and profession
Time to complete degree	Teaching quality, productivity, innovation	Proportion of inter-disciplinary activities
Fraction engaging in practical training e.g., co-op or internship	Effectiveness of student advising	Rate of temporary exchange of persons with industry and government
Fraction engaging in undergraduate independent study or research	Publication and other dissemination of knowledge	Level of, and trends in institutional support
Fraction participating in education abroad	Institutional, professional and public service	Demand for institutional efforts (applications, inquiries, etc)

Employment patterns and salaries after graduation	Successful collaborations and mentoring	Character of internal and external review processes
Graduate school admissions and fellowships	Contributions to continuing education	Alumni engagement
Student satisfaction and employer satisfaction	Internal and External honors and awards	Stature in the profession and in society
	Faculty career satisfaction Networking	

(Source: Technical Education: Current Status and Future Directions Vol I: R Natarajan, Icfai Books 2005)

FOUNDATION FOR ENGINEERING EDUCATION

There are many schools but the question remains 'is the learning really taking place? While we marvel at the flash in the pan performance by our students either in America's spelling Bee contest or by ex IITians in the Silicon Valley, a former NCERT Chairperson Krishna Kumar calls this a Lotus Syndrome – We admire the lotus but ignore the mud around it. China's adult literacy rate hovers around 94% compared to India 74% while China's expenditure on education as percentage of GDP is actually lower than India's. Strangely even in India there has been a decline in percentage GDP spending on public education from 4.2% in 1999–2000 to 3.8% in 2008–09; and the glaring short fall of 1.5 million teachers says it all on the quality of our school products. The year 2011–12 being crucial for RTE (Right to Education) implementation, only less than half (Rs. 21000 cr) the sanctioned budget (Rs. 48000 cr) has been released with another meager Rs. 7 crore, in the pipe line. Yet another tale comes in the form of poor teachers where, of 7.5 lakh candidates who appeared for CBSE's (Central Board of Secondary Education) all India teacher recruitment test only 93000 cleared, and even of those recruited, one would find hardly anyone doing their assigned job properly despite the starting salary being

Rs. 23000/- pm after VI Pay Commission report. The problem is of lack of accountability and the assured life long job security. Most of the teaching work is assigned to the lowly paid para teachers (Shiksha Mitras) who are more regular than the permanent teachers despite high pay disparity as they get only Rs. 3500/- pm. In some rural areas 'the proxy teachers' take over just to mark the attendance for the regularly absentee permanent teachers. Last but not the least malady, that is so peculiar to our country, where teachers and schools are put to any use other than education i.e. teachers always on one form of election duty or the other, like census duty etc and schools serving as temporary camps for villagers during floods or natural calamities, or as temporary camps for police personnel, or for political rallies etc, you name it, the school is meant for it and the teacher is the nearest government servant or the errand boy, to undertake any task. Under these circumstances neither the teacher nor the student will have any interest in education or in learning and if at all it is there, it would be purely exams or marks oriented and not with an eye on seeking of knowledge per se.

Our outlook towards education must change to start with, teaching profession must revert to its golden days of Gurukul and finally Govt must ensure investing of 9 to 10% of the GDP on education with suitable control and monitoring mechanisms in place, to improve the quality of school education as the same forms the very basic foundation for further and higher education.

Quality is never an accident.
It is the result of an intelligent effort.
There must be a will to produce superior things.

– John Ruskin

TQM in Engineering Education and Role of Faculty

Total Quality Management (TQM) is an integrated system where in all quantitative methods and human resources are brought together to improve all processes within the organization on a continuous basis so as not only to meet but to exceed the expectations of the stake holders. The concept as far as engineering education is concerned is to ensure imparting of quality education, which covers the entire gamut of activities starting from admission of a student to his quality performance in the actual work environment, as a graduate engineer. TQM broadly covers the following activities.

- Entry barriers in terms of transparency in admissions, strictly as per merit/rules framed from time to time
- Sound infrastructural arrangements (Specially Labs and Workshops)and proper maintenance
- Updated and contemporary curriculum
- Creation of a healthy academic ambience and rigor
- Extensive use of technology in teaching
- Continuous industry interaction and orientation of syllabus to their needs
- Innovation in teaching, evaluation and insistence on application of knowledge
- Involvement of parents/guardians in problematic student management
- Adequate compensation, recognition and rewarding of best performers
- Open door policy in all activities
- Heavy emphasis on research by faculty
- Role clarity and accountability at all levels
- Discipline and code of conduct for all in all aspects of functioning
- Laying stress on development of employability skills among students, and their personality development through co-curricular activities
- Rigidity in conduct of examinations
- Effective student feedback system and follow up
- Establishment of an Alumni Network and maintaining interface

- Mechanism to place students in the industry and also to seek feed back on their performance
- Interface with regulatory bodies/universities/professional bodies for faculty development
- Student/faculty exchange programs with well known institutes of excellence both in India and abroad
- Motivation of all employees through effective HRM practices

Thus the list can go on.... and anything that adds value to the education delivery system can be a part of the TQM. If continuous improvement is the heart and soul of TQM, faculty forms its back bone. It can be seen from the above that faculty has a role to play virtually in every activity. Even the non teaching (support) staff have a major role to play in TQM as it is they who keep the infrastructure geared up all the time. No TQM can even be conceived without sound infrastructure in place and most of the engineering colleges in the private sector have been found wanting in this area with many of them having make shift or temporary arrangements. On the other hand state owned colleges start on a very well organized infrastructure and somewhere down the line the maintenance aspects get neglected.

With regard to training of faculty in various areas pertaining to TQM, management bodies of the colleges need to be proactive in identifying the facilities and sponsoring the faculty to attend the programmes. AICTE, ISTE, IITs, NITs and other premier institutes have been doing excellent jobs in contributing to the professional advancement of engineering faculty through various initiatives. Many engineering colleges conduct exclusive 2-3 days workshops in TQM from which the faculty can benefit. Just as they say 'learning is best done by doing it', every engineering college must necessarily include at least one TQM workshop in their annual calendar.

4

The Milestones Crossed

The journey, not the arrival matters

– T S Eliot

HRM as an operationally important function is gaining its strong foot hold in the industry and is slowly inching its way to the strategy table too. It's relevance in the education sector is barley making its presence felt as a 'concept' as most of the entrepreneurs or managements of educational enterprises still see it more as an avoidable cost centre rather than as a vital developmental tool. It's this tendency that has probably weaned away the HR/OB authors from touching the very sensitive topic of HRM in engineering colleges and refrained them from undertaking any active research in the area. However it is gratifying to note that plenty of research has been undertaken on 'Engineering Education' in our country as such, and issues of HR interest pertaining to faculty did get highlighted in these works more by default than by design. Though the literature on HR processes in the institutions of higher learning is scanty, a pioneering effort was made by two researchers way back in the year 1995 itself.

David Warner and Elaine Crosthwaite in their edited version of the book 'Human Resource Management in Higher and Further Education (SRHE: The Society for Research into Higher Education & Open University Press 1995) emphasized on the following:

- The HR professional must operate at top level. The HR strategy must form part of overall organizational strategy (Elizabeth Lanchberry)

- A diverse workforce is essential to contribute a valuable range of skills and abilities (Rebecca Nestor)
- The institutions must encourage lifelong learning by mentoring and coaching (Jennifer Tann)
- The educational environment does not differ significantly from the commercial world in so far as a large proportion of its success will come from the contributions of a well-motivated workforce bound together by effective communication (Jo Andrews)
- Performance Management is not satisfactory to maintain achievements of the past or to enable staff to improve their future performance (David Bright and Bill Williamson)
- The advantage of using executive recruiters to assist with academic appointments are numerous (Diana Ellis).

However a notable and a remarkable contribution to the field of engineering education in our country was made by Shri R. Natarajan, Former Director IIT Chennai and Former Chairman AICTE through his various works and publications. To mention a few of them

- "Technical Education: Current Status and Future Directions" Volumes I, II and III by the Icfai University Press : 2005
- "Contemporary Issues in Engineering Education" Ed: R Natarajan, MP Ravindra, and R Hariharan, Macmillan: 2008
- "XXI Century Priorities in Engineering Education" Ed: R Natarajan, and M Anandakrishnan, Macmillan: 2010.

  In the 'Technical Education' series the learned author discusses the following

- The role of technical education in national development
- Academic Quality in Technical Education with special reference to ranking and accreditation etc.
- Evaluation of Student Performance and Students' evaluation of Teacher's Performance

- Role of teachers, their accountability and work ethics
- Performance Appraisal of teachers
- Industry Institute Interface
- Societal Responsibility of the institutions
- Current Status and Future Directions for Indian Engineering Education
- International perspectives on Engineering Education

The compilation on 'Contemporary Issues in Engineering Education' basically deals with the acute shortage in the availability of quality (Ph D) faculty and the use of technology to improve upon the learning management systems and processes. An effort was also made to reduce the gap between the curricular offerings and the actual job requirements.

It's heartening to note that an exclusive section was devoted in the book 'XXI Century Priorities in Engineering Education' to HRD (Human Resource Development) highlighting the following:

- HRM Strategy is for implementing clear and definite mission with vision
- Suitable mentoring mechanisms to be in place to motivate people to undertake research
- Continuous industry – academia interface to implement 'employability enhancement' programs/initiatives
- Measures to identify the inherent talents of the individuals so that one takes up the study based more on one's aptitude rather than by force
- Intertwining of knowledge, people and technology in a Knowledge Based Economy (KBE) to train students who can adapt to the changes taking place in the environment
- Introduction of more industry relevant electives so as achieve a win-win situation both for students and the industry

In a study (involving 300 teaching and non teaching members) titled 'Leveraging Human Potential through HRM Strategy: A case study of Jawarharlal Nehru Technological University (JNTU), by Prof Y Venkatrami Reddy the then Vice Chancellor of the University, the following were the findings

- Multiple roles played by the faculty in handling various academic and non academic assignments (80%)
- Freedom to choose career path including shifting to industry (90%)
- Importance of flexible and transparent organizational culture (60%)
- Global opportunities through variety of exposure and diverse experiences to the faculty (60%)
- Adequate and satisfying performance recognition measures (90%)
- Existence of Value Based Work Environment (80%)
- Openness (58%) and Continuous learning and growth opportunities (90%)
- Incentives for best performers (100%)
- Strong Social Security and Employee Welfare (70%)
- Performance oriented Organizational Climate (70%)
- Visibility, transparency and accessibility of the leaders (68%)
- Job Security and stability (100%)
- Well defined organizational philosophy and culture (80%)
- Work systems and right procedures in place (82%)
- Freedom to work and innovate (90%)
- Career growth through structured and flat organization (70%)
- Exhaustive induction and orientation program (95%)
- Strong academic governance and citizenships (75%)
- Opportunity for cross functional and locational mobility (84%)
- Focused training to meet the demand of high performers (70%)

(The percentage figures in parenthesis indicate the affirmative response of the respondents during the survey)

The University as per the above study report made a modest beginning in the year 1972 with an annual intake of 500 students, rose to become one of the largest technological universities in the country registering a massive growth in the annual intake of students reaching a figure of 80,000 and the secret of all such phenomenal success is the HRM strategy of the university which by itself is a tribute to HRM function as such.

In the Draft Final Report titled 'Engineering Education in India' prepared by Rangan Banarjee and Vinayak P Muley, study sponsored by Observer Research Foundation, Energy Systems' Engineering IIT, Bombay Powai, Mumbai (Sept 2007) the following HR related issues were dealt with

- Faculty Student ratio
- Attracting Quality Faculty
- Incentivizing the Performance
- Faculty Quality Improvement Programs
- Industry Linkages
- Societal Linkages
- Journals, Conferences and Academic Press
- Faculty Publications and Research output
- Faculty Compensation etc

By far, a comprehensive discussion on engineering education of our country can be found in the work of Professors Gautam Biswas, KL Chopra, CS Jha and DV Singh titled "Profile of Engineering Education in India': Status, Concerns and Recommendations" (Narosa Publishing House Pvt Ltd, 2010). The following are the highlights as far as HR issues are concerned

- Challenges being faced by engineering education
- Ethics in Engineering practices
- Faculty Shortages
- Improvement of teaching and learning processes
- Research, and Development

- Industry –Institute interaction
- Governance and Management of Engineering Colleges

Prof R Natarajan in his edited book 'International Accreditation Perspectives' (An ISTE Publication-2012) highlights proceedings of the International Conference on Accreditation - 2011 through various papers presented in the conference, whose main objective was to spread the awareness of quality assurance and accreditation systems as a concept for our engineering education. Yet another volume of twenty six papers has been brought out by Prof R Natarajan and Prof NR Shetty under the title 'Multiple Stakeholder Perspectives of Higher Education' (an ISTE Publication-2012) concerning engineering discipline mainly dealing with quality and accreditation, faculty development, faculty and student attributes, research, technology enabled engineering education, and leadership development etc.

All the above mentioned literature and studies indicate one single factor that a good teacher produces a good student and also a good citizen for the country. The review further outlines that no exclusive effort was ever made to deal with the 'HRM of the faculty' as such except in case of JNTU at Hyderabad, whose HRM strategy was reported to have paid rich dividends. There is apparently no reason why others cannot bench mark their HR practices with JNTU and derive similar or more benefits all in the interest of the engineering education in our country which by itself is an economy differentiator.

PART II

5
HRM in Engineering Colleges: A Faculty Related Perspective

Ideal teachers are those who use themselves as bridges over which they invite their students to cross, then having facilitated their crossing, joyfully collapse, encouraging them to create bridges of their own

– Nikos Karantzakis

People have always been central to organizations and people management defined as the organization's ability to attract, develop, motivate and retain talented employees, forms an important criterion in deciding the success or failure of an organization. It's the people 'the human resource' that drive organizational performance through their skills and capabilities along with other resources like money, machinery, materials and information. All things being equal it is this human resource which enables the organization to create more economic value than its competitors, what we may otherwise call as 'competitive advantage'. This is as true for any educational enterprise as it is for a commercial outfit.

To quote the words of M. Ananda Krishnan "The educational system should foster the development of our young men and women into individuals with an openness of mind a sense of self confidence, a capacity to meet challenges, a capability of creative thinking. It should produce good citizens of the country having an ethos for intellectual honesty and high ethical values. They should be leaders and innovators of tomorrow to handle the challenges of life with a spirit of community and a concern for fellow beings and the environment."

It's time educational institutions start considering people as competitive advantage and not as cost centres. How well they are managed forms the core issue as any mismanagement is likely to drive people away from the organizational objectives.

In the wake of preponderance of engineering colleges across the country mostly in the private domain, each one needs to preserve its own competitive advantage with 'people centric know how' which includes the skills and abilities embodied in its members, forming the set of 'core competencies' for it. The IITs and NITs have thus carved a niche for themselves which very few private players could emulate. The resource based view model highlights the need for the faculty's knowledge base to be of value, be gifted with rare qualities making it difficult for others to imitate, ensure optimal utilization and be subjected to periodic review and evaluation for its relevance with the changing times.

It's time one takes a look at the very basic concept of 'teacher' who for too long has been accepted as the 'one who just teaches some one' without laying much emphasis on 'educating some one' which implies that a teacher's role does not end merely with the good academic performance of his student but extends beyond in imparting of quality of mind and character too. In simple terms a teacher has the dual responsibility of transferring accumulated knowledge to a student and the next, to develop overall personality of the student so that the society gets a good citizen. This concept assumes all the more significance in the case of an engineering faculty as they turn out young engineers who build the nation. These teachers are expected to acquire knowledge, create new knowledge through continuous study and research, and then disseminate this knowledge to the younger generations. To that extent they become 'knowledge workers' as they keep creating and adding value to their profession. The knowledge so possessed and created shall become the intellectual property of the institute.

The profession of teaching has been a time honored activity, considered a noble one at that due to its closeness to concepts like, intellect, intelligence, knowledge and wisdom. The professional responsibility resting on the shoulders of the teachers is enormous as they virtually build the nations and shape the destiny of the future generations. It's a tough call as teachers also need to become worthy of emulation by their students in all walks of their future life. A teacher can be called truly professional when he possesses subject knowledge, knows its applicability, feels responsible and accountable for his actions and inactions and finally when he becomes a role model for his students. It may be apt to recall an extract from the editorial of a Bangladesh News Daily 'The Independent' which says of the teachers as "*Teachers, specifically those serving in the highest seats of learning, are to be the representatives of the finer values of our society, including a missionary dedication to their task of shaping the future of the country as well that of our younger generation*".

For a teacher it does not suffice merely by telling or teaching (mediocrity) as he needs to explain things (good teaching), then demonstrate (superior teaching) before reaching the inspiring stage of becoming a great teacher (A Harvard teacher's view).

A professional teacher deserves to be not only labeled as knowledge worker but also to be treated as such. The knowledge system of the professional faculty consists of two independent sub-systems of 'delivery' and 'gestation'. Through delivery he strives to utilize his ready to use competencies in his day to day work, while through gestation he works towards learning, practicing and assimilating knowledge of futuristic developments in science and technology field.

Dr Howard Gardner, a professor of Harvard University and the father of the theory of multiple intelligences (verbal-linguistic, logical-mathematical, visual-spatial, bodily-kinesthetic, musical, interpersonal intrapersonal, and naturalist) argues that different children learn differently based on the type of intelligence and the active genes they possess. He challenges the very basic notion that there is only one standard kind of human intelligence and argues further that a person's intelligence can neither be quantified nor it can be judged by the marks he or she gets in a traditional examination. A food for thought, at least for engineering education in our country.

Characteristics of Engineering Faculty as Knowledge Workers

Keeping the ever growing relevance of engineering education in the national developmental process, it is imperative to examine certain typical characteristics of a technical teacher (engineering faculty)

- They invest substantial time, effort and resources in acquiring skills in their chosen area of discipline
- They are enthusiastic about using the acquired knowledge and seeking new knowledge
- They are analytical in their outlook and teach others to be so
- They crave for reward and recognition for their achievements
- They are keen to work on new and challenging assignments
- They tend to be more committed to their profession than to the organization they are working for
- They value autonomy, professionalism and innovativeness

Expectations of Engineering Faculty

With the growing demand for 'quality faculty' in a highly competitive environment, every faculty member tends have his own set of expectations from the career he is pursuing. They may sound simple but are very important nevertheless.

- Suitable compensation to maintain a decent living standard
- Conducive work environment with sound infrastructural facilities

- Guaranteed self esteem
- Self development and career progression facilities
- Equality and fair play
- Enthusiastic and responsive set of students to teach
- Encouragement for innovation and creativity
- Value adding experience through research and training
- Recognition and appreciation for good work and guidance from the seniors

Finally a teacher irrespective of the field he is in has the onus of owning the responsibility of ensuring human development as his contribution to the society in terms of turning out good citizens for the country. Confucius' scholarly definition of a teacher sums it up all.

"When a superior man knows that causes which make instruction successful and those which make it of no effect, he can become a teacher of others. Thus in his teaching, he leads and does not drag: he strengthens and does not discourage: he opens the way but does not conduct to the end without the learner's own efforts. Leading and not dragging produces harmony; Strengthening and not discouraging makes attainment easy; Opening the way and not conducting to the end makes the learner thoughtful. He who produces such harmony, easy attainment and thoughtfulness may be pronounced a skillful teacher".

6
Acquisition (Recruitment & Selection)

The true measure of a man is not how he behaves in moments of comfort and convenience, but how stands at times of controversy and challenges

– Martin Luther King Jr

No activity can be, rather should be taken up without proper planning, more so in the case of acquiring human resources for any organization. That way Human Resource Planning (HRP) as a 'process of anticipating, and making provision for the movement of people into, within and out of an organization' (Bohlander & Snell 2005) forms the very basis for all other HRM activities in the organization. Once the requirement of manpower is determined then the managements need to look into various means of attracting people (recruitment) and picking up the right ones (Selection). Recruitment involves identifying various sources of prospective employees including internal and taking steps to make them apply for jobs, aim being to get as many aspirants as possible. Large 'applicant base' would enable proper selection of right man for the right job. More often than not, it has been observed that educational institutions tend to resort to 'panic hiring' or 'crisis recruiting' just before the onset of the academic session. Due to the intense competition, and heavy demand for the qualified faculty, engineering colleges mostly in the private sector leave themselves with no choice but to compromise on the standards of intake. As against this, recruitment and selection as on going process if taken up on round the year basis will definitely result in some good quality faculty joining the institution. This way one can avoid selection error (selecting a wrong person) and rejection error (rejecting a right person) both of which cost the organizations dearly.

Some theorists like Michael Armstrong (2006) have widened the scope of Human Resources Planning to include the entire gamut of HRM i.e. to attract and retain people with relevant skill sets, anticipate surpluses or deficits, develop workforce to meet the changing needs, optimize the people utilization and institute an efficient retention strategy, and he suggests formulating a resourcing strategy based on the following parameters

- Requirement of faculty in each domain area/department
- Skill set required, Vs existing and gaps if any
- Plans to meet the gaps in skill sets, develop or extend the skill set base
- Plans to attract, develop and motivate and retain the faculty
- Weeding out the low skilled/poor performers

RECRUITMENT

Departmental Committees

A consensual approach to deal with any important activity is by far the best method, and most of the educational institutions have committees for various activities. Likewise even in an engineering college it is advisable to have a committee at each departmental level, the constitution of which could be as under

- Presiding Officer/Chairperson: HOD/Dean

  Members : 1. Senior Faculty (Ph D)

  2. Faculty

  Member Secretary- HR Manager of the Institution

The scope of these departmental committees could be widened to deal with various other issues apart from recruitment and selection, such as

- Research
- Seminars/Conferences
- Intellectual resources addition
- Consultancy assignments
- Academic audit
- Curriculum review as per university regulations
- Accreditation norms
- Admin/HR
    - Welfare & Grievances
    - Discipline
    - Incentives, rewards and promotion
    - Any other issues assigned by the management.

The proceedings of the committee shall be recommendative only in nature. Certain important and sensitive points recommended for attention of the Committee

- Head of the institution is the final approval authority
- HR Manager to form part of the committee only for dealing with HR issues. For other issues, he/she could be replaced by a suitable faculty member
- The committee's recommendations shall be in conformity with the laws of the land/regulations of the AICTE or UGC or of the University to which the college is affiliated to, whichever is applicable and HR Manager shall apprise the committee accordingly.
- The committee may at its own discretion decide the periodicity of their meetings and inform all concerned well in advance.
- The members of the committee may be rotated periodically, so as to ensure objectivity
- While dealing with any issue concerning one of the members, the concerned member may be replaced by another faculty from the department

Recruitment Methods

Before the methods are discussed, it would be pertinent to make a mention of the general departmental hierarchy in an engineering college

- HOD/Dean
- Professor
- Reader/Associate Professor
- Faculty Member/Senior Lecturer
- Faculty associate/Lecturer
- Research Associate/Teaching Assistant/Junior Lecturer

  (Variations from the above may be there as per local conditions)

In our sample survey, 'advertisement' mode appeared to be the most popular method of attracting talent in engineering colleges. A brief discussion on some recruitment methods.

Advertisements

Most of the advertisements one comes across are purely routine type with some of them carrying, glaring spelling and grammar mistakes. These convey a poor image of the institution and a good and well qualified faculty would always remain away from such institutions. The advertisement more in line with the perception of the aspirant designed most innovatively, must be run in a right medium at a proper place and time so that it attracts maximum attention and response from the prospective candidates.

E-Recruitment

By far the least expensive and the most appropriate method of recruiting people on 'all through the year' basis rather than limiting the activity to the academic session starting season only. Since all engineering colleges have their own websites (which of course need to be managed properly and updated regularly), there could be a link titled 'Faculty-Positions/Vacancies' where all the details of requirements could be specified for seeking on line responses from the desirous candidates. Alternatively job placement websites could also be used for posting the jobs available in the college.

Unfortunately none of the engineering colleges surveyed by us adopt this method of recruitment while 95% of the organizations in the US reportedly go for it.

Consultants

They provide all back office services like, inserting an advertisement, sifting through the applications, carrying out preliminary interview and final short listing etc.

Though this reduces the administrative work load of the engineering colleges, but it comes with a heavy cost and budget conscious organizations may not be able to afford it. Secondly a HR consultant looks at the issue more from his business angle than from the institution's actual requirement point of view. Moreover, the host institution's name is not revealed till the last minute which may prove detrimental to the image of the college in the long run. This method has not been found to be very popular among the conventional engineering colleges as revealed during our survey.

Employee Reference

After 'advertisement' method, employee reference mode of inducting new faulty into the system has gained prominence all over. This is a safe, cost effective and a very convenient method in the sense, no employee would refer a bad case knowingly. Organizational culture and working environment play a major role in promoting this method and a suitable incentive to the referee based on the performance of the 'referred' would result in a win-win situation.

Informal Methods

Engineering Colleges could consider the following informal methods of attracting quality faculty

- Identify quality faculty during seminars/conferences conducted both in house and outside
- Publication and circulation of 'Newsletter' of the college among academics and industry
- Participation in 'job fairs' and display of publications of faculty
- Undertaking PR (Public Relations) exercises like ' TV Talk Shows', FM Radio interactions, and appearing in Education supplement Features of major news papers etc
- Frequent interaction with industry through 'guest lectures' and 'industrial visits' etc

Visiting, Adjunct or Part Time Faculty

Certain shortages of qualified faculty can also be met by having Visiting or Part Time/Adjunct Faculty, who possesses necessary skills and expertise. They could be either from the academic fraternity having retired from the active service life but having penchant for teaching, or from the industry who manage to take time off from their regular work life to pursue academic interests. Some engineering colleges in the private sector do exercise this option. A visiting faculty may teach a specified number of sessions per week while an Adjunct or a Part Time Faculty may attend the college for a specified number of days in a week, all depending upon mutual convenience and requirement. This system has certain advantages

- Add value to the teaching since they come from diverse backgrounds
- Cost effective and win-win arrangement
- Industry faculty assist in industry interface
- Academic background faculty are normally 'experts' in their area

However there is a need to look at the flip side too while appointing faculty through above route

- Relationship with the institution is purely transactional lacking loyalty and sense of belongingness
- Academic rigour may be compromised due to other commitments and lateral moves
- Play no role in institutional image building process
- Intellectual property of the institutions shall be at risk
- It would be appropriate to recall the words of a well known academician in this regard

"One needs to understand the distinction between availability of human resources to serve as faculty and recruitment of good faculty. The observation that is often made is that good faculty is scarce. But, at the same time, the question arises why should we expect to get readymade good faculty only? Why cannot we have a slight shift in our stand by owning up the responsibility to develop the available willing resources that are not only willing to serve as faculty but have a distinct potential for development into good faculty. Careful screening and selection of the right person, therefore becomes crucially important. Merit should not be compromised at any cost. Qualifications should not be relaxed. Good faculty is not necessarily available with the industry (U Dhar 2004)."

SELECTION

Wisdom is meaningless until your own experience has given it meaning, and there is wisdom in the selection of wisdom

– Bergen Evans

Engineering colleges have a mandate to provide quality technical manpower to the nation who would contribute to its developmental process. In order to do that they need to equip themselves with quality faculty by selecting right people. Broad policy as enumerated by experts.

"In as much as freshly recruited faculty member has a career span of over 30 years in an engineering college, it is important that great care is exercised in the recruitment and selection of the faculty. The recruitment process should ensure that the competence, talents and interests of the prospective faculty match the needs and requirements of the institution. It is wiser to fill positions at the level of assistant professor/lecturer. This policy promotes good morale in the institution, since positions at higher academic levels are filled through promotions from the ranks" (R Natarajan 2005).

The above mentioned author, engineering teacher and scholar has outlined the multiple functions of engineering teachers in one of his works (Technical Education: Current Status and Future Directions- Vol II The Icfai University Press 2005). Briefly they are

- *The Teaching Function:* Teaching activity should make the student convincingly learn the subject including its applicability, get satisfied with the learning, and finally become keen to learn further or take up an activity in the area
- *The Research Function:* Favourable research climate fosters faculty development and acts as a motivator for a good teacher
- *The Consultancy Function:* The experience and knowledge gained in consultancy assignments can become good teaching tools
- *The Admin/Management Function:* Teachers need to broaden their functional skills by taking up roles in academic administration and various committees, etc
- *Professional Bodies:* Teachers must take active interest in all the activities of professional bodies to enhance their knowledge and develop networking
- *Continuing Education Activities:* Teachers must conduct seminars, and participate in them by presenting papers, and give lectures at various fora on varied subjects to broaden their knowledge base and build the image of the institution

In addition to above, any teacher specially of professional institutions like engineering colleges has the following roles to play which are more implied than specified

- Development of soft skills, sound character and ethical outlook among students
- Keen interest to convince students on the applicability of the knowledge imparted and develop entrepreneurial skills among them
- To be a role model for the students

Commerce without morality and education without character is dangerous

– Mahatma Gandhi

Various stake holders involved in the process as the engineering colleges go about in developing engineering personnel for the country are

- Management of the Institution
- Students and Parents
- Faculty and Admin staff
- Industry
- Regulatory Bodies, and Universities
- Society in general

Expectations of each group are interlinked with those of the others. As can be seen 'faculty' is the most important link connecting all the other groups 'as he ultimately is the one responsible to send out an useful, productive and competent engineer into the industry/society'. To that extent he needs to possess knowledge, its application skills and finally the personality development skills but unfortunately most of the faculty and the management to a certain extent feel that mere possession of 'adequate knowledge' and an ability to impart it are good enough for a teacher. A mind set which needs to change, the sooner the better.

It would be pertinent to take a look at the delivery and feedback model involving all the above stake holders

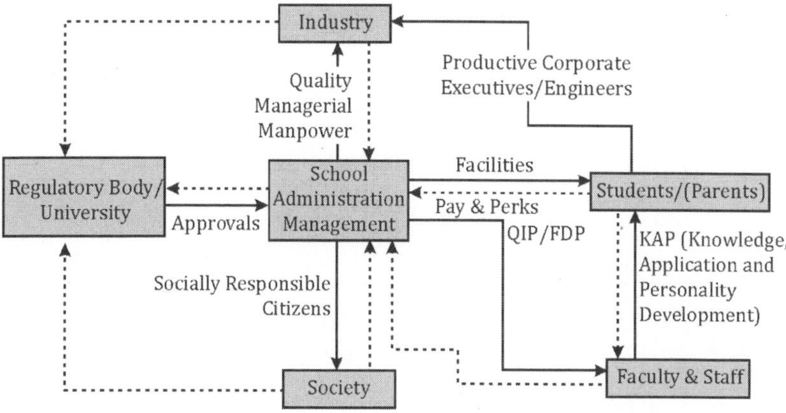

Delivery (⟶) & Feedback (- - ➤) Model of a typical engineering college

(Source: The Business of HR in Business Schools: VRK Prasad – Viva Publishers 2011)

> *"The education of the global citizen, one who will be comfortable, visiting, working, and living in diverse countries is the responsibility of the academia*
>
> – Lundstrum & Schuster *(1988)*

Based on the above discussions, a competency based HR model for faculty selection and retention is suggested as below

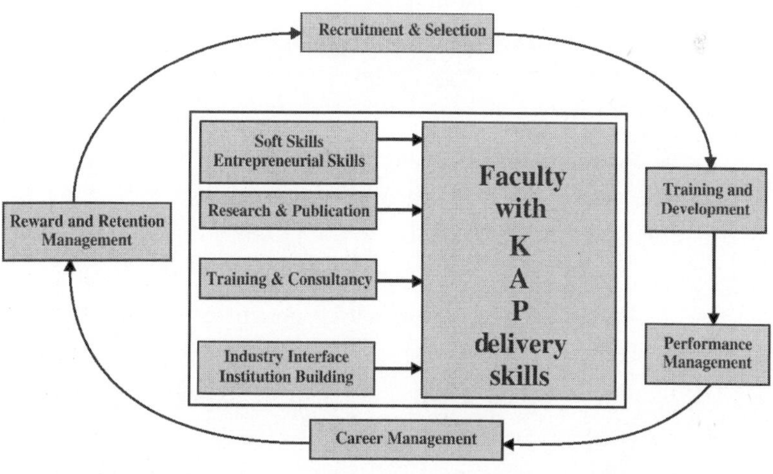

(KAP-Knowledge, Application and Personality Development)

(Source: The Business of HR in Business Schools: VRK Prasad – Viva Publishers 2011)

Selection Methods

Following selection methods could be considered for implementation.

- **Application Blanks and Preliminary Screening**

  A college can design its own application blank depending upon the type of information that it needs to solicit from the candidates. Generally they deal with the biographical information of the candidate like education, work experience and specialized training received etc. The R & S (Recruitment & Selection) or the departmental committee sifts the received application forms by comparing them with the key criteria in the job specification, position wise and sorts them into three groups: good, average and poor. The 'average' category could be gone through again to assess if they can be graduated to 'good' list. Thus a short list of good potential candidates is made.

  In view of the criticality of selecting a quality faculty who is both eligible from qualifications and experience point of view and suitable from performance on the job, view point, the committee could ask the candidate to submit a hand written note along with the application blank which could be called the 'Hiring Template for an engineering college Faculty'. It basically deals with the ideas and perceptions of a candidate about the profession he is planning to pursue. The candidate could be asked to respond in bullet point form (a minimum of five and a maximum of ten) for each question. The aim of this document is three fold.

- Social structure of a human being can be studied through his hand writing, and graphology as a selection aid is being used extensively all over the world. (Fowler 1991 a)
- As per Psychologists the handwritten answers to various questions generally indicate the candidate's general tendency towards the job, with not many deviations.

- Acts a short listing tool for the R & S committee.

(**Note:** The doubtful responses if noticed could be cross checked during the actual interview)

The template is suggested to be on the following lines.

A model of 'Faculty Hiring Template' for an Engineering College

1. What is your concept of an engineering faculty.
2. Name the books and the authors you normally refer in your functional area.
3. How do you plan to deal with difficult or weak students.
4. What soft skills you think you possess.
5. How do you propose to impart knowledge and its application to students.
6. What is your idea of 'character building' of a person.
7. How do you plan to maintain industry interface.
8. How can you contribute to' institutional image building' process.
9. What are your views on 'Engineering Education in India'.

(Source: The Business of HR in Business Schools: VRK Prasad – Viva Publishers 2011)

Demo Lecture

This is a high validity test for assessing person job fit, where a candidate is made to take an actual class either for a live set of students or for the R&S committee, or for both. Short listed candidates could be put through this test. Certain aspects to be kept in mind for adopting this method

- Candidate to be given the topic by the department and adequate time to prepare for it
- To be given adequate time for actual presentation making the necessary facilities available.
- Preferably to be conducted in the presence of R & S Committee, in a live class room like a normal class and a random feed back from the students could also be considered
- A grilling question and answer session at the end is essential

Interviews

Based on the outcome of Demo Lecture a candidate is interviewed by the R & S Committee. Again this is a high validity test for a person job fit with moderate validity for assessing person group or organization fit. Structured interviews are suitable so that the committee members are well in sync with each other. This is an ideal platform to cross check the responses of the candidate for various questions of the 'HR Template' suggested above.

Further preplanned standard questions to test the depth of the subject knowledge and of contemporary thoughts could be asked which would highlight the specific skills and competencies relevant to the job. A situational or behavioral questions like "what if a student behaves rudely...." could also be asked to probe into student management capacity, of the faculty.

Psychometric Tests

The purpose of these tests is to provide an objective means of measuring individual abilities or characteristics. They enable the selectors to decide the extent to which a person shall be successful on the job. Smith and Roberstonson (1986) define a psychological test as "a carefully chosen, systematic and standardized procedure for evolving a sample of responses from candidates which can be used to assess one or more of their psychological characteristics with those of a representative sample of an appropriate population". The 'HR Template' suggested earlier more or less meets this requirement well before getting on to the actual selection process.

- On successful completion of the above stages a candidate may be seen by the institutional head where an unstructured interview could take place resulting in either approval or rejection of the R & S committee's recommendations.

Reference Checks

Once a candidate has been found to be suitable for a job offer, reference checks are made from his previous employers, or co workers with or without the knowledge of the candidate. Most of the time only a positive image of the candidate comes up during such checks as the lists are generated by candidates themselves. Hence it is suggested to carry out a discrete check from past students and unlisted colleagues if possible at college level only as hiring of professional agencies for this would be a very expensive proposition.

Summing Up

By and large one of the serious problems that is being confronted in the engineering education field today is the shortage of talented and qualified faculty, and the critical need to take up proper planning and resorting to various methods of attracting and selecting most suitable ones as against the most eligible. Eligibility is the meeting of quantitative requirements of a job while suitability deals with the actual delivery on the job. The entire R & S activity is depicted in the flow chart below.

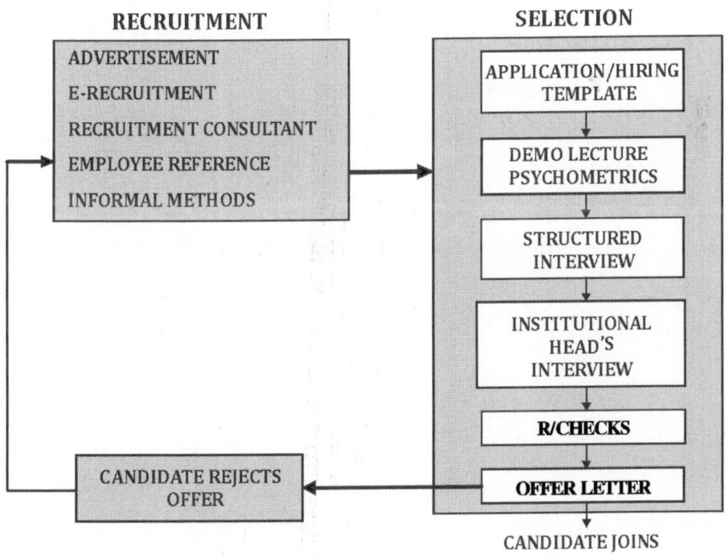

R & S Chart for an Engineering College

(Source: The Business of HR in Business Schools: VRK Prasad – Viva Publishers 2011)

7
Development through Training

Continuous effort – not strength or intelligence – is the key to unlocking our potential

– Liane Cardes

Training is the methodical process of imparting relevant skills and competencies in the employees and no organization can afford to remain away from this essential activity. The aim of training is to equip the employees with the skills required to meet the demands of the current job on hand while 'development' has a long term objective in the sense, an effort is made to broaden the employee's skill set base to meet the future requirements. But the fact that any training leads to individual development in the first place needs no debate. A trained manpower is an asset for any organization and engineering colleges have the onerous responsibility of 'training the trainers' i.e. training their faculty so that they are successful in meeting the institutional objective of imparting quality education to their students. Development of a faculty can take place through various measures, but training is the most essential and critical one as it boosts his self confidence, prepares him to face challenges and finally sets the pace to scale greater heights in acquisition of knowledge. Hence it may be proper to consider 'training' more as an individual developmental tool rather than as an academic obligation.

The need for in-service training was visualized as back as 1949 when University Education Commission observed "A teacher to keep alive and fresh should become a learner from time to time.

The training for in-service teachers is essential in view of explosion and obsolescence of knowledge". This particular need gets rightly emphasized further in the words of late Peter Drucker who in his essay 'The Age of Social Transformation' argues that "we are in the midst of the most extreme societal changes in the recorded history. These changes now in turn pose a challenge to the way we manage our institutions, where there is a strong need to unlearn, learn, and relearn as to how to adapt to the new environment on a continuous basis". Thus the importance of training needs no further emphasis.

It's a strange phenomenon that young faculty in engineering colleges are mostly fresh from their colleges having acquired masters or doctoral qualifications without any formal training in teaching per se unlike the school teachers who get adequate exposure in teaching techniques in their B.Ed or M.Ed programs before moving on to the job. Thus the need for training in case of fresh engineering faculty is an inescapable requirement. Yet another reason is the acute shortage of quality faculty in the colleges with only limited institutions offering masters or doctoral programs. Fortunately some groups with number of educational institutions under their fold have their own Faculty Development Institute (Sharda Group of Institutions), Faculty Training Academy (BS Abdur Rahman University, Chennai) while government has done its bit in having its own institutions like National Institute of Technical Teachers Training and Research, Chennai and Centre for Developing Advanced Computing (C-DAC) offering both short and long term courses/training pertaining to various technical and non technical areas. Yet another initiative comes in the form of ICT Academy of Tamil Nadu (ICTACT), Chennai which is a consortium of Govt. of India, Govt. of Tamil Nadu, and Confederation of Indian Industry, established in 2009 to train the higher education teachers of Tamil Nadu in the areas of Information and Communication Technology (ICT) with the ultimate aim of benefitting the student community. Most of the engineering colleges of Tamil Nadu having become members of ICTACT are reportedly deriving the benefits of training programs offered.

With some private operators like Nettur Technical Training Foundation (NTTF) South India/Tamil Nadu is reasonably well positioned to train engineering faculty in comparison to other areas of the country. Deriving the benefits from the advanced technology, IIT-B (Indian Institute of Technology-Bombay) in Dec 2009 started beaming training capsules to engineering faculty through satellite and around 1300 teachers from about 300 colleges across India are understood to have benefitted from the first two workshops itself. Around 94.87% teachers trained thus gave a feed back saying that the training made them teach better. An ambitious target of training over 12000 teachers in the next few years has been set. The project is an MHRD (Ministry of Human Resource Development) initiative who has also launched National Program in Technology Enhanced Learning (NPTEL) through which teachers from private engineering colleges are getting trained to make better use of technology for improving their teaching skills and also in getting exposed to MIT and Stanford Coursewares. (The Hindu, Hyderabad, May 30, 2012). Close on the heels of this, comes yet another initiative in the form of a degree in engineering and training from the IITs for the untrained faculty members across engineering colleges in India. This will be a part time on line masters degree in engineering education which will focus on research aspects with an objective of training 6000-7000 faculty members each year reaching a figure of 30000 at the end of 12th Five year plan. The demand for faculty in engineering colleges is expected to go up by 70% by the year 2020 to match the number of students pursuing technical education which has more than doubled in the last five years alone and likely to go up further. Govt is also reportedly planning to start a three year program to encourage post graduate students in IITs to opt for teaching profession. Even industry is also being urged to start teacher training programs so that teachers ensure the students become employable and are trained to meet the specific demands of the industry.

AN IDEAL ENGINEERING PROFESSOR

It is pertinent to discuss the results of an informal survey by the International Federation of Engineering Education Societies (IFEES) and the Student Platform for Engineering Education Development (SPEED) on the skills and the competencies of the ideal engineering professor undertaken in the Fall of 2009 through 88 responses among students (56 from 14 countries), faculty/deans (28 from 5 countries) and industry members (4) by Lueny Morell and Jennifer De Boer. The results are in the table below.

Table 1. Top Five Attributes of Respondents by Category

Faculty/ Dean	*Industry*	*Students*
1. Knowledge of engineering fundamentals, engineering practice and technically competent	1. (Tied) a. Engineering experience b. Current (up-to-date) in research, publishing c. Multi-culture sensitive, inclusive of people and environments	1. Inspiring, motivating 2. Prepared and knowledgeable (including real-world knowledge) 3. Committed to teaching and helping
2. Effective teacher 3. Strong sense of professional responsibility/ ethics 4. Influential Communicator 5. Mentor	2. (Tied) a. Superior technical depth and savvy b. Highly networked and open minded; fosters collaboration and teamwork c. Superior communication skills (articulate in context of non engineering disciplines, especially business) d. Able and willing to nurture curiosity, fostering bold, innovative thinking; receive and formulate big and tough questions	4. (Tied) a. Effective communicator b. Person of integrity

Source: 'Multiple Stakeholders Perspectives of Higher Education' Ed: R Natarajan, NR Shetty: Macmillan 2012 Page 99

There is little or no doubt that engineers of the future will be requiring new skills and competencies and the faculty needs to possess them himself in the first place to be able to impart to the students. In yet another survey (Engineering 2020), both industry and academia have disagreed with the assertion that the current engineering education is sufficiently flexible to adequately meet the needs of the Twenty First century engineers. Lack of attention towards engineering teachers themselves seems to be the key outcome of this.

> *"Engineering...is an unforgiving and demanding environment...for students to succeed as engineers, they must acquire skills that go far beyond theories, simulations and exam-taking.... there is absolutely no substitute for the hard-edged technical and business skills that are required to bring products and projects to market".*
>
> – Bernard M. Gordon, founder of NeuroLogica Corp., founder & former chair of Analogic Corp., and co-founder of Epsco Inc.

Most of the engineering teachers confine themselves to the conventional mode of teaching i.e. lecture method (87% faculty even in the US adopt this), rarely interacting with students (delegate it to juniors) either inside or outside the class room. Further, they have very little or no practical industry experience with the result their teaching goes without conviction. At best he can present himself as a good teacher, a researcher, a paper publisher/presenter, a patent submitter, or even as a role model for a student planning to pursue a career in academics. But how many such cases would one find in a class room? Very few, most others wanting to work as 'engineers' in the field. The authors of the paper 'What are the Desired Engineering Professor's Skills' (Lueny Morell and Jennifer De Boer) have rightly pointed out that 'engineering education' needs to have both engineering and education as the principal components while we have only 'education' component today.

> *'We are continually trying to find better, cheaper, safer, less harmful and more energy-efficient ways to do things. Yet, we don't use an engineering approach to engineering education!"*
>
> – Karl Smith, Purdue University

No doubt present engineering faculty's understanding of what engineering profession in reality is all about, is rather debatable as he never practiced it, nor is he aware of the business constraints while suggesting a solution to a given problem. They were never exposed to multi-disciplinary or multi-national teams, and fortunately teachers cannot be faulted as most of them get hired for their intellectual pursuits in terms of teaching, research and publication and not for industry exposure. Over emphasis on Ph D made one lose sight of the practical experience requirement in engineering education. The foundation for ideal engineering education was laid in 1894 itself by Professor WH Burr, Professor of Civil Engineering at the Columbia College School of Mines in New York which is as valid today as it was back then. To quote the distinguished teacher:

> *"The method of instruction to be pursued in the school which affords the ideal education in engineering must be of such a character as to yield the best results with the least amount of unproductive labour to the student, and at the same time, train him in the ways of vigorous and independent thought. Dry and lifeless text book recitation work yields by itself little enough that is desirable, while the pure lecture method is equally unsatisfactory. The one is uninteresting routine and utterly ill adapted to the development of mental fertility and strength, while the other involves a mass of misdirected labour on the part of the lecturer, which, without supplementary exercises,*

leaves the student to shift for himself, without producing much of any result.
The main purpose is to convey instruction, and it should be done in such a way as to induce the student to do his own thinking. No instructor can justify himself in merely puzzling the student with grotesque problems, or in harassing him with abnormal difficulties, but on the other hand, the student should be made constantly to feel himself a working part of the system, and that he cannot, without serious loss to himself, take a mere passive part."

– Prof WH Burr, 1894 from
an article of his, published in the first
proceedings of the then newly formed Society
for Promotion of Engineering Education

Based on all the above discussions the learned authors Lueny Morell and Jennifer De Boer have developed a model for 'an ideal engineering professor' which is depicted below:

Fig. 1. The Ideal Engineering Professor?

Source: 'Multiple Stakeholders Perspectives of Higher Education'
Ed: R Natarajan, NR Shetty: Macmillan 2012 Page 101

Having discussed at length on the various attributes for a faculty it is essential to highlight the actual areas of faculty training and the institutions' need to focus upon. Briefly the **Focus Areas** are

- Contemporary Teaching Methodologies
- Student Management and Teacher Being a Role Model
- Question Paper Setting
- Evaluation Methods/Techniques
- Subject Knowledge Acquisition: Current Trends
- Creation of Knowledge through Research and Publication
- Curriculum and Content Development for various programs and courses
- Communication skills and related soft skills
- Application of knowledge through practicals and projects
- Periodic Industry Exposure through sabbaticals and summer internships of students
- Supervision and Assessment of Student Projects
- Fundamentals of General Management, business and finance basics
- Environmental awareness
- Conducting surveys/workshops/seminars/conferences
- Global Business Awareness
- Training Need Analysis
- Training to train others
- Training in Consultancy
- Training in conducting Industrial tours and outbound training
- Conduct & Controller of Examination
- Accreditation Methods & Ranking Surveys
- Academic Co-ordination
- Orientation to Changing Trends in Engineering Education
- Institution Building Activities
- Training for Leadership positions
- Alumni Activities

> *"The faculty should not be restricted to teaching only. The multiple roles of a teacher in a professional institution cannot be undermined. A teacher cannot end up as a class room operator……. Involvement in institution building activities should be facilitated Continuous faculty development should be seen as an investment, not as an expenditure"*
>
> – U Dhar 2004

It is generally seen that training needs are rarely or never assessed (assessed only in 50% cases as per a survey by American Society for Training and Development – ASTD) and training is carried out more as a routine or even to meet minimum laid down stipulations of the regulatory bodies like the AICTE/UGC or the universities to which the colleges are affiliated, than to impart any worthwhile knowledge. Even worse is a case where general training is offered across all the trainees irrespective of their individual needs which totally defeats the very purpose of training. A well organized system of assessing the individual needs either through student feed back, personal interviews, counseling or even through performance appraisals (PA) should be put in place before designing an appropriate training program, for the needy lot. Motivation of the faculty to get trained is very essential. Various institutions call the training so imparted as FDP (Faculty Development Program), FTP (Faculty Training Program) or even as QIP (Quality Improvement Program) etc. In addition certain other training forms that could/ need to be adapted are

- Induction/Orientation Training
- Refresher Training
- Workshops/Teaching Workshops for Fresh Teachers
- Industry training

Induction/Orientation Training

This training is given to a new entrant to familiarize him/her with the culture of the institution and the role one is expected to play in enhancing institutional effectiveness. Extra emphasis is to be laid on teaching methodologies and student management for fresh graduate teachers. The training period depending upon the number of freshers could vary between one and two weeks.

Refresher Training

Generally conducted to ensure that the faculty remains updated knowledge wise in their functional areas. They could be conducted departmentally by having one of the experienced faculty members as the resource person. This is an ideal and the least expensive form of training where faculty members prepare and present papers among their peers first and gain confidence to present them in bigger fora. The departmental faculty could plan to meet once in a fortnight or in a month for the purpose.

Workshops

This is a 'learning by doing' model focused on a single theme to establish a proper link between theory and practice. If conducted properly this could become the most interesting, stimulating and challenging form of training and may last over 2 to 3 days.

Industry Training

Engineering faculty with virtually no industry exposure, have a big handicap in convincing the students on the application of the knowledge imparted by them. Hence it is essential that they are deputed to the relevant industry during summer vacations or to supervise students' projects from the company premises itself. (Practice School –BITS). This industry experience gives them plenty of confidence in disseminating knowledge to students which otherwise would be reduced to a mere vocal delivery of facts and figures.

FDP/FTP/QIP

They could be conducted in any or all of the areas discussed in the foregoing (Focus Areas) and wherever it is not possible to conduct these programs internally, institutions could take the benefit from any other institutions discussed above. Alternatively the faculty's development could also be ensured by

- Sponsoring faculty for training conducted by other well known institutions like IITs, IIITs, BITS, NITs etc
- Sponsoring faculty to attend seminars/conferences and giving incentives for presenting papers
- Reimbursing cost of undertaking M.Phil or Ph D programs
- Sparing faculty for undertaking field work during research
- Providing infrastructural facilities in terms of wide band internet, software packages like SPSS and on and off line libraries, etc
- Incentives for publication of articles/research papers/ books
- Mentoring and Coaching by senior faculty

FACULTY IMPROVEMENT MEASURES

Lately a very innovative and highly motivating initiative has been undertaken by AICTE through '**1st AICTE-CII Survey of Industry linked Engineering Institutions & AICTE Awards for Institutions and Faculty**' to critically examine the areas like governance, curriculum, faculty, infrastructure, services, entrepreneurship and innovation and placements. The survey will lead to giving awards to Best Engineering Institute stream wise and over all, and of all recognizing and rewarding the 'best faculty' in various disciplines of engineering (Times of India, Hyderabad, Jun 08, 2012). The awards will be given during 4th Global Higher Education Summit on 8th Nov 2012. (AICTE- CII University Industry Congress).

Yet another Quality improvement related measure comes from AICTE again in the form of 'AICTE Quality Promotion Schemes

2012–13' for granting financial assistance to institutes/candidates in the following areas

- Research Promotion Scheme (RPS)
- National Co-ordinated Project (NCP)
- National Facilities in Engineering & Technology with Industrial Collaboration (NAFETIC)
- Modernization and Removal of Obsolescence (MODROBS)
- Entrepreneurship Development Cell (EDC)
- Industry Institute Partnership Cell (IIPC)
- Travel Grant (TG)
- Seminar Grant (SG)
- Faculty Development Program (FDP)
- Emeritus Fellowship (EF)
- Career Award for Young Teachers (CAYT)
- Visiting Professorship (VP)
- AICTE –INAE Distinguished Visiting Professorship (DVP)
- National Doctoral Fellowship (NDF)
- Quality Improvement Programme (QIP Centres)
- Research Park (RP)
- Innovation Promotion Scheme (IPS)
- PG Scholarships (Institutions shall apply)

(Source: The Deccan Chronicle, Hyderabad Jun 30, 2012).

Lately AICTE has come up with yet another unique initiative to train 10000 faculty of AICTE approved institutions in winter and summer schools programmes of MHRD/AICTE under Faculty Development Scheme for the year 2012–13 making them mandatory for all government and government aided institutions. Other institutions can also conduct them on voluntary basis. Training is to be conducted in four levels covering teaching methodologies, upgradation of knowledge base, advanced and emerging technologies and in preparing faculty for academic leadership roles, and responsibility etc.

(Source: The Deccan Chronicle, Hyderabad Aug 08, 2012).

The faculty catering for the 'millennial' generation (born between 1982–2002) need to develop their teaching skills in exploratory and experiential methods, personalization and customization, multimedia systems, and finally in being flexible in schedules. These skills can be acquired by having an open mind in attending conferences, workshops and seminars, and conducting research projects and collaborating with colleagues from other institutions (Mohan & Janardhan). Apart from the University System (central, state and private) research intensive organizations like Indian Institute of Science, Bangalore, Institute of Mathematical Sciences, Chennai etc about 38 such publicly funded research institutions and laboratories promote applied research under the patronage of CSIR (Council of Scientific and Industrial Research) of which many are recognized for university doctoral research work. Certain other avenues through which faculty development/improvement can be ensured are (R Natarajan)

- Consultancy
- Industrial Sabbaticals, Collaboration and even short tenure employment with the relevant industry
- Multi disciplinary and integrated approach to teaching
- Reduced institutional barriers
- Encourage team teaching
- Recognition of cross disciplinary skills in rewarding
- Promoting research culture through incentives, sabbaticals and special leave for research etc

Experts like Gautam Biswas, KL Chopra, CS Jha, and DV Singh in their treatise 'Profile of Engineering Education in India; Status, Concerns and Recommendations' have highlighted the following issues with regard to improvement of faculty

- Benefit from the QIP (Quality Improvement Program) Schemes organized by AICTE from time to time by taking up M Tech and Ph D programs in reputed institutions and revert to parent institution on completion

- Take up short term refresher courses conducted by AICTE, and ISTE as and when announced
- A move is afoot to increase the number of M Tech seats from 400 to 2000 and that of Ph D from 100 to 1000 respectively and to extend the opportunity to the faculty of private engineering colleges also
- A provision to do away with the mandatory sponsorship in case of private engineering college faculty has also been recommended
- Facilities to undertake research in national laboratories by the academic faculty under the guidance of the research professionals working in those laboratories
- Derive maximum benefit from Virtual Technical University (VIRTUAL TECH) apart from the web based programs/ lectures prepared by IITs, IISc for the National Programme on Technology Enhanced Learning (NPTEL) programs
- Revival of Summer Schools in various disciplines

QIP is an ongoing and very successful initiative of AICTE and is going a long way in meeting the requirements of the faculty in handling the present lot of hyper active, knowledgeable tech savvy and finally a little impatient for results, type of students. Yet there is a plenty of room and requirement to extend the scope so that much larger percentage of private engineering college faculty are also necessarily brought under its purview. Needless to say that private operators are sending out more number of engineering graduates into the environment than the state owned ones. All that it requires is 'the right will and the aptitude' on the part of the concerned faculty, to improve while there is really no dearth of facilities in our country.

CONCLUSION

That the engineering professor today needs to be application oriented needs no further emphasis and continuous interaction with the industry should become a regular feature among the academia. The institutional leaders may draw a road map of administrative strategies as per NAE Engineering Report 2020 and follow it in letter and spirit.

> *" A knowledge economy is one that relies intensively on human skills and creativity, the utilization of human intellectual capital supported by life long learning and adaption, the creative exploitation of existing knowledge and extensive creation of new knowledge through research and development"*
>
> – Anonymous

8

Morale and Motivation

Motivation is the art of getting people to do what you want them to do, because they want to do it

– Dwight D Eisenhower

One hears of the terms morale & motivation being used more often than not, in the armed forces because of their critical importance in various operations. With all principles of management owing their origin to various battles fought by the armies across the world over centuries, today's organizations facing stiff competitions are more or less similar to battle grounds; and engineering colleges are no exception. Morale is the state of mind while motivation is making people 'want' to do what you want them to do. If one does not hear these words being mentioned frequently in day to day working life then they are assumed to be sound and good. (DD Eisenhower). Morale and motivation are closely interlinked like the two sides of the same coin; If people are motivated enough, then it naturally leads to sound morale among them. Basically it is the 'motivation' aspect of HRM one needs to address, and then morale will take care of itself.

Human beings are selfish by nature and they are motivated only when their self interests are taken care of.

Before a person attempts to do a particular thing, he will always be anxious to know the outcome. One tends to repeat the behavior if the consequences are to his liking and not otherwise. Again one's likes and dislikes are based on one's needs.

Responding and meeting the needs of a human being is what we may call as motivation in simple terms. On a Monday morning if an employee can feel and say 'thank God it's Monday' then sure enough the people are highly motivated and possess sound morale. All the same it is pertinent to look at the various needs that motivate a person which could be either psychological (recognition hungry) or physiological (money & comforts)

- Needs for Achievement, Power and Self Esteem
- Needs for autonomy and affiliation
- Needs for safety and security
- Needs for equity and justice

Above needs are to be essentially converted into various organizational activities to ensure that faculty of an engineering college are motivated enough to deliver the quality goods expected out of them. Briefly they are

- Creating a conducive organizational climate
- Ensuring a compensation package matching with the efforts and the background of the faculty
- Proper Performance Appraisal Systems to ensure rewarding of merit and hard work
- Providing adequate avenues to undertake 'Research and Consultancy' by the faculty both as a self growth measure and also to promote organizational interests.
- Ensure faculty maintain continuous Industry Interface
- Put in place a proper 'faculty retention strategy'

It is relevant to quote Gallup Survey on what (workers) employees actually want from their managers/managements in order to get motivated

'Focus on me

Care about me

Hear me

Help me feel proud

Help me review my contributions

Equip me
Help me see my value'
Help me grow
Help me see my importance
Help me build a mutual trust
And
Challenge me'

ORGANIZATIONAL CLIMATE

'The way we do things here' is what we could simply call as organizational climate which is more apparent and obvious in the front office rather than the organizational culture which is more in the background defined by beliefs and value systems. The interpersonal relations between the employees shall constitute what we could call as 'Social Capital' of the organization which is as important as any other capital in today's scenario. This social capital in turn contributes to the organizational climate in terms of perceptions that individuals have of, how their local work unit is managed and how effectively they and their day-to-day colleagues work together on the job (Burke and Litwin 1992). Organizational climate is further identified by the kind of cohesiveness and team spirit people exhibit, the trust that exists among them, the autonomy and functional freedom they enjoy, the supporting and recognizing environment that prevails, and finally the justice and fair play the managements shower the employees with.

Certain measures that ensure conducive organizational climate are

- Role clarity for each and every faculty
- Recognition of Good and hard work through matching rewards
- Open communications and accessibility of the top management
- Fostering team work

- Careful & proper change Management
- Social interactions to develop family like atmosphere in the institution
- Participation in both pains and pleasures (official and personal) of the employees
- Promote sense of equality, fairness and justice
- Implementation of a proper code of conduct and general sense of discipline among staff
- Conduct of regular morale/satisfaction surveys or 'culture audits' by professional agencies

Ensuring a sound organizational climate in an educational institution is very important as students tend to very closely observe the activities happening in the institutions and also their faculty members and form their opinions and attitudes purely based on these observations.

> *Creating a fun, challenging and empowered work environment in which individuals are able to use their abilities to do meaningful jobs for which they are shown appreciation, is likely to be a more certain way to enhance motivation and performance – even though creating such an environment may be more difficult and take more time than simply turning the reward lever*
>
> – Pfeffer 1998

COMPENSATION & REWARDS

> *It is entirely possible to design a reward system that motivates people to work and satisfies them while at the same time contributing to organizational effectiveness*
>
> – Ed Lawler in *Treat People Right*

The statement 'money constitutes the single most important gratifier and motivator' needs no debate though non monetary incentives do play a significant role alright. A compensation package consisting of both the above elements is what people receive in exchange for their work or contribution to the organization. A standard compensation policy in an engineering college should ideally be linked to organizational objectives, performance standards and to motivate the faculty to do their best. The organizational objectives in the case of an engineering college can be briefly summarized as

- Quality of students passing out
- Acceptance of the students by institutions of higher learning for research work
- Absorption of students by the industry
- Performance of students on the job
- Performance of students on further higher education

Colleges can put suitable systems in place to collect data on above mentioned objectives through alumni networks, industry linkages and by undertaking surveys etc.

Pay for Performance is the most important part of the compensation management for any organization as it has to reward people

- For their value addition to the organization
- Differentially for different outputs
- To attract, and retain them
- To enhance their performance
- To achieve organizational objectives/goals
- To develop and nurture good working relations

Total reward (Michael Armstrong 2006) is the combination of financial and non financial rewards, which are further classified as 'transactional' and 'relational' awards. Faculty members are generally more concerned with transactional awards which constitute the following

- Pay for properly evaluated job at market rates

- Special/variable pay
- Employee benefits/perks
- Allowances and Incentives

The relational awards cater to the psychological needs of the faculty and engineering colleges need to be at their innovative best to meet them.

Compensation Strategy

Since pay represents a reward received in exchange for an employee's contribution, it is essential that he perceives it as commensurate with his efforts and equitable in relation to others. More so because the pay has a direct bearing on the status and the standing of the individual in the society. As a simple thumb rule either AICTE or UGC scales (revised in the year 2009) could be considered for implementation across the board by engineering colleges to obviate the main grouse among the faculty today. Most run of the mill engineering colleges have been observed to be leaving a lot to be desired in this aspect where in the freshly inducted faculty are reportedly being paid pathetically low salaries. If an engineering college decides to have its own 'compensation system' in place as is generally seen among the private sector, it should be comparable to either AICTE or UGC scales with only marginal variations. The Grade Pay introduced in the above scales could be introduced as Special or Variable Pay in private colleges so as to motivate the faculty to take on additional responsibilities etc. The Compensation package should also cater to the following employee benefits

- Leave of all types and encashment facility
- Statutory provisions in terms of PF and Gratuity
- Medical and Health care benefits to self and family
- Conveyance and Leave Travel Allowance
- Magazine/Periodicals Allowance
- Research Grants
- HRA and CCA
- DA linked to CPI

Pay for performance extends beyond normal pay through incentives that are earned through extra efforts put in over and above the routine work. Incentive plans establish a basic threshold that a faculty must cross to be eligible to receive an incentive. Again this incentive could be either financial in terms of cash or non financial in terms of additional leave for research or nominating for a seminar abroad, etc. Following are the areas where the faculty could be considered for grant of incentives

- Research, for taking up themselves or for guiding others
- Publication of articles/research papers/books
- Presentation of papers in seminars and for winning awards in them
- On being rated as the 'Best Teacher' by students
- Share in the consultancy and 'in company' training remunerations received from companies
- Loyalty incentives for continuously serving the college for stipulated periods like 3,5,10 or more years
- Teaching additional courses over and above the specified load
- Handling any additional assignments on academic/admin areas
- Referring new faculty members for induction into the system
- Developing Course material
- Supervising projects of students over and above the 'specified load'
- Conducting technical workshops/seminars/conferences
- Question paper setting and answer book evaluations

Compensation must adequately reward the employee's past efforts while motivating him to continue doing well in future too. A private university in South India has inserted an advertisement in 'The Hindu' (Opportunities Feature), Hyderabad edition on 14th March 2012 for faculty at various levels where in the following benefits were listed

- 6th Pay Commission pay scales
- EPF & Gratuity
- Encashment of Earned leave/40 days of vacation leave/90 days of maternity leave
- Special casual leave to attend workshops/conferences/seminars and to present papers
- Sponsoring faculty to present papers in India and abroad
- Quarters/Accommodation in the university campus
- Computing/Internet facility (100 Mbps with Wifi) in University Staff Quarters
- Incentive to the faculty for publishing papers in National/International journals
- Bus facility from city to the University and back
- Advance increment for Ph D degree holders
- Personal Pay for Network branches
- School Education for employees' children in the university campus
- Faculty Members are encouraged to take up Research and Consultancy
- Mediclaim Insurance/Accidental Policy for employees and dependants
- Medical facility in the University Campus
- Special incentive of Rs.30,000 pm for Ph D holders

Compensation is a critical part of employee-employer relationship and employee considers it as a measure of his personal success. Hence there is a dire need for a systematic and consistent approach for measuring and recording the relative worth of a job and consequently that of a faculty performing it. The reward system must satisfy and motivate people to put in their best in furtherance of organizational objectives. Depending upon the environment, the college managements may at their own discretion decide to keep the pay of the faculty as a confidential matter known only to the person concerned. However the pay & allowances structure with details of eligibility to get a particular allowance/incentive must be available on the college website to be known by all.

PERFORMANCE APPRAISAL

> *An organization is like a tune it is not constituted by individual sounds, but by their synthesis*
>
> – Peter Drucker

Performance Appraisal is a major constituent of Performance Management which by itself is a developmental process as against the 'appraisal' which is evaluatory in nature. Performance appraisal is an important organizational mechanism through which an employee's contribution to the organizational effectiveness is measured against pre set standards. The success of an engineering college would largely depend upon its ability to accurately measure the performance of its faculty so as to objectively optimize or manage it. It might sound difficult to define the tasks of faculty being intellectual in nature but definitely some clearly measurable standards can be set. The charter of duties of a faculty include basically the teaching loads apart from self developmental academic pursuits and finally the institution image building activities, with each one being as important as the other. The concept of performance appraisal is relatively new in educational institutions where career advancement facilities exist but more by default than by design. Any effort to introduce proper HR systems is generally frowned upon by the managements with the plea that educational institutions are not corporate entities, on the other hand if performance of a faculty is important in furtherance of the organizational objectives, so is the appraisal part of it to separate wheat from the chaff.

Before we proceed further on appraisal related issues it would be prudent to highlight the performance management aspects which would generally cover the whole gamut of activities during a faculty's stay in an engineering college. Generally they are

- Job description
- Proper selection to ensure person-job fit
- Setting of performance standards
- Adequate training for proper performance on the job
- Sound performance appraisal and review systems
- Proper reward and recognition systems
- Provision of growth opportunities
- Exit interviews and follow up

As can be seen the most important and essential steps in any PMS are, setting the standards, facilitating and managing the performance round the year and carrying out periodic reviews with a well designed tool (Michael Armstrong, 2006).

It could be quite some time before the educational institutions resort to establishment of PMSs, nevertheless the PA mechanism needs to be put in place which to the extent possible must avoid the following pitfalls (Townley, 1989)

- too controlling
- restricted to review of past performance
- incongruent with organizational needs
- too much of paper work
- tends to be more evaluatory and judgmental than developmental
- tends to be subjective

Performance Standards & Students' Feed back

Making it clear to an employee as to what is expected of him during the course of his employment with the organization is an essential feature of the employment contract. Faculty and management of an engineering college are no exception to this basic tenet though it was generally observed that these expectations were limited to mostly verbal and informal ways, of communication. Ideal situation would be to reduce them to a simple written communication clearly specifying the expectations so that the faculty goes about in meeting them in his own methodical way. This facilitates easy measurement and subsequent assessment of his performance. Student's feed back should not be the sole criteria for assessment as most of the colleges under our study seem to prefer, as many other factors contribute as much to a faculty member's performance. Colleges can use the mnemonic SMART (S-specific and clear objectives, M-Measurable, A-Achievable, R-Relevant and T-Timeframe) to set the performance standards. However a suggested format is attached at Annexure I to this chapter, and colleges can modify it to suit their individual requirements.

One of the most important aspects of a teacher's job is to satisfy the students with his knowledge dissemination or simply teaching skills. The concept of formal rating of teachers by students came into existence in 1920s at the University of Washington. Now how does faculty go about in satisfying the student with his instruction.

A study indicates the following (R. Natarajan 2005)

- To motivate the student to learn and assimilate
- To demonstrate to the student with appropriate practicals as to what he is expected to do further in his working life
- To organize the teaching to the liking of the student so that he understands the significance of learning
- To provide the student necessary opportunity to judge his (teacher's) performance

Different rating scales are in use by various universities across the world as far as students' evaluation of their teachers' performance is concerned. Depending upon the number of students a particular faculty is handling a simple format could be designed to obtain students' view points on the subject knowledge, teaching capabilities and student handling capabilities of the faculty. A suggested format is attached at Annexure II to this chapter. Students may not be insisted upon to reveal their identities, and the choice be rather left to them.

A cautionary approach to adopt this method is highly essential to ensure that both the students and the faculty do not misuse, or manipulate it. Two or three evenly spaced on line 'feed back mechanism' is more likely to be objective and true.

Status & Career Prospects

'Status needs are important in the hierarchy of needs' (Maslow) is a statement which needs no further debate as every faculty member puts in his best to climb the career ladder. Hence the performance appraisals must cater for rewarding the good performers by satisfying their psychological needs (promotion etc) as much as they do for their physical needs (pay and monetary incentives). A clearly defined promotion policy is an essential component of any PMS, and engineering colleges must institute one, which should lay down the eligibility conditions for each level so that a faculty member could put in commensurate efforts to reach it. A suggested format is attached at Annexure III to this chapter.

Introspection & Self Appraisal

A Faculty being a 'knowledge worker' also deserves to assess himself or carry out introspection which may or may not be in tune with other forms of assessment of his performance. Before the actual performance appraisal is undertaken by his superiors/HOD, he/she could be asked to furnish a simple one page assessment of his own performance during the period under review, in relation to the performance standards set for him/her. This is likely to remove certain unintentional gaps in the actual performance appraisal of the faculty, while also serving as an effective upward communication tool through which a faculty could also convey his developmental needs to the management. Yet another suggested format to undertake this exercise is attached at Annexure IV to this chapter.

SUMMARY

Performance Appraisal is the most critical and sensitive feature of HRM of any organization more so that of an educational institution.

The objectivity, fairness, and openness are the essential ingredients. Honesty, truthfulness and courage of conviction without any personal biases on the part of the rater play a significant role in ensuring the fairness of the system. The appraisal should be need and fact based, kept confidential between the rater and the ratee and finally one should neither depend upon others' views nor delegate the act of assessment to anybody while carrying out the performance appraisal of a ratee. Finally the rater should have observed the performance of the ratee from very close quarters before undertaking the actual assessment exercise. Prof R Natarajan in his paper 'Fundamental Concepts of Performance Appraisal' (Technical Education: Current Status and Future Directions Vol II - Icfai Books 2005) highlights the following to alleviate the pitfalls in the rater's personal bias

- Appraise the performance and not the personality
- Each appraisal factor to be considered as a separate entity without mixing it with other factors
- Should not be based on one particular incident/event.
- Tendency to rate all as 'same' to be avoided
- Extreme ratings to be duly justified

Mutual trust is the life line of any appraisal system and engineering college managements need to ensure its existence so that no faculty member loses faith in the system. Every college can design its own format to carry out the performance appraisal of its faculty; however a suggested layout of the same is attached at Annexure V to this chapter. Colleges may modify it to suit their convenience.

Performance appraisal dates back to 1842 Federal Government in USA, when a law was enacted by the congress to review the performances of basically the clerical category, but soon it spread to cover all and sundry in all organizations. In India, while it is an essential operational function in both the government and the industry it is still in its nascent stage in education sector. Surprisingly most of the private engineering colleges this author got in touch with do not have a proper and formal performance appraisal system in place, where only students' feedback is used to judge faculty's performance. The HOD has little or no say, while a faculty must get the opportunity of working under a senior faculty/HOD that could guide him throughout and also apprise him of his weaknesses and explain the methods to overcome. Students' feedback at best may bring out the grey areas. Then there is an ample need to set the performance standards right in the beginning so that faculty members chart out their course of action to reach a particular objective. Finally the performance appraisal shall serve its intended purpose only where evaluation is followed by developmental measures. Interesting UGC regulations published vide The Gazette of India dated Sep 18, 2010 (Part III-Sec.4) stipulate issue of Service Agreement (Para 16.1) at the time of recruitment of faculty, where self appraisal or linked Performance Based Appraisal System (PBAS) is expected (Para 16.2) to form part of the said agreement.

Self Appraisal

A little boy went into a drug store, reached for a soda carton and pulled it over to the telephone. He climbed on to the carton so that he could reach the buttons on the phone and proceeded to punch in seven digits. The store-owner observed and listened to the conversation: The boy asked "Lady can you give me the job of cutting your lawn". The woman replied, "I already have some one to cut my lawn". "Lady I will cut your lawn for half the price of the person who cuts your lawn now." Replied the boy. The woman responded that she was very satisfied with the person who was presently cutting her lawn. The little boy found more perseverance and offered "Lady I will even sweep your curb and your side walk, so on Sunday you will have the prettiest lawn in all of North-Palm Beach, Florida". "Again the woman answered in the negative. With a smile on his face the little boy replaced the receiver. The Store-owner who was listening to all this, walked over to the boy and said "Son... I like your attitude; I like that positive spirit and would like to offer you a job". The little boy replied, "No thanks I was just checking my performance with the job I already have. I am the one who is working for that lady I was talking to.

– Source not known

Annexure I

ABC Engineering College
(Department of ....)

Date: ....

To
Prof: ....
Designation: ....

Dear Prof

Performance Standards for a Faculty Member

1. Your performance review period starts on .... and ends on ....
2. You are expected to ensure the following minimum performance standards during the above period of review.
   - Teach a minimum of .... Courses/term/semester/year
   - Earn a minimum student feedback of .... on a scale of ....
   - **Publish** — Number
     - Technical articles –
     - Research papers –
       (National/International Journals) –
   - **Present Papers in**
     - Local/Regional/National Seminars –
     - International Conferences/Seminars –
   - **Industry Interface**
     - Organize Guest Lectures –
     - Arrange Projects for students –
     - Supervise/guide students' projects –
     - Arrange placements for students
     - Take up consultancy assignment –

- **Institution Building (As applicable only)**
    - Edit a news letter/magazine/journal –
    - Organize seminars/conferences –
    - Organize media coverage –
    - Refer 'quality' faculty for the college –

3. Take up Doctoral Program/Post Doctoral Program/Guide research scholars.
4. All the above are intended to serve as guidelines only and your proactive and innovative approach to add value to students and to the institution will always be welcome.
5. Kindly sign on the duplicate copy and return it to us as a token of your acknowledgement.
6. Wishing you all the very best in all your endeavours.

Yours Sincerely

XYZ ....
HOD (Dept of ....)

Annexure II

ABC Engineering College

Suggested Format for Feedback on Faculty by Students

			Knowledge & Teaching Skills*					Professional Characteristics*					
S. No.	Faculty Name	Course taught	Subject knowledge depth	Coverage of syllabus	Communication & Presentation skills	Application Techniques	Evaluation Methods & Fairness	Classroom Management	Innovative approach	Interactive & Inclusive	Questioning & Listening	Rapport with students & Mentoring skills	* All ave's/avg.

Note: *Each parameter is to be marked by the student on a scale of 10 and averages of all students feedback are to be taken to arrive at final averages (A faculty is expected to have a minimum grading of 6 to be considered for retention).
Caution to be exercised in 'extreme' feedback cases, by taking student's attendance, conduct and performacne in the class into consideration.

*Outstanding– 9-10
Excellent-8-9
Good-6-7
Barely satisfactory-4-5
Unsatisfactory-3 or below

Both Optional { Signature of the Student
Name of the Student..................................

Date:................................

Annexure III

Suggested Hierarchy Model and Promotion Criteria in a Typical Engineering College

Designation		Recommended Eligibility
• Junior Lecturer or Teaching Assistant (TA) Research Associate (RA)	:	M Tech with min two years work experience and academic bent of mind: To be put as Understudy to a Faculty Member/Senior Lecturer
• Faculty Associate (FA)/ Lecturer	:	Two years as Junior Lecturer/TA (starts actual teaching)
• Faculty Member/Senior Lecturer	:	Two years as FA/Lecturer
• Senior Faculty Member/ Assistant Professor	:	Three years as FM/Senior Lecturer
• Associate Professor/ Reader/Associate Dean	:	Three years as SFM/Assistant Professor and Ph D
• Professor/Deputy Dean	:	Three years as Associate Prof./ Reader and Ph D
• Senior Professor/Dean/ HOD/Vice Principal/Deputy Director	:	Three years as Professor or Associate Dean
• Director/Principal	:	Five years as Senior Professor or Dean/HOD or 20 years of overall teaching and admin experience with a Ph D.

Note: Designation and eligibility conditions may be altered for candidates with exceptional qualifications and experience both in academics and industry depending upon the individual merits. As a general guideline, a consistently good performance for a period of two/ three years may be considered essential for promotion to next level.

Annexure IV

ABC Engineering College

Self Assessment by Faculty

For the period from .... to ....

(To be read in reference to Performance Standards set on ....)

Name of the Faculty: .... **Department: ....**

Designation: .... **Date of Joining: ....**

In pursuance of the performance standards set for me vide Department of .... letter dated .... I assess my performance during the period from .... to .... as under.

1. Self Developmental Activities undertaken during the review period. (like additional qualifications acquired or projects undertaken, etc.)

2. I achieved all the performance standards set for me.

   Or

   I could not achieve all the performance standards set for me and the shortfalls with the reasons there of are mentioned below.

   Or

   I exceeded the performance standards set for me the details of which are given below (additional achievements only)

3. I rate myself as under (Outstanding – O, Excellent – E, Good – G, Satisfactory – S, Unsatisfactory – US). (Use abbreviations)

   - Teaching Capabilities and Subject Knowledge ☐
   - Student Interface and Classroom Management ☐
   - Research and Intellectual Capabilities ☐

- Industry Interface
- Institution Building
- Personal Attributes
- Overall Grading

4. I request for the following professional development facilities.

5. I have the following suggestions to make.

Date: ....

Place: Signature of the Faculty

....

Remarks by the Assessing Authority

I do/*do not concur with the above self-assessment (score out 'not applicable').

....

Signature of the Assessing Authority

Date ....

*'Do not concur' instances should be duly supported.

Annexure V

ABC Engineering College

Faculty Annual Review and Development Report

For the Academic Year/Period ....

Emp. Code: .... Name of Faculty Member: ....

Department: .... Designation: ....

Assessment is to be done in the light of performance standards set, and the self-assessment form submitted by the faculty. It is the performance that is to be reviewed and not the person per se. Developmental Aspects are not to be lost sight of.

Grading as per Self Assessment By Faculty

1. Your assessment of the faculty member: (Tick one)

A. Teaching Capabilities & Subject knowledge

❒ Outstanding ❒ Excellent ❒ Good

❒ Satisfactory ❒ Unsatisfactory ☐

B. Student Interface & Classroom Management

❒ Outstanding ❒ Excellent ❒ Good

❒ Satisfactory ❒ Unsatisfactory ☐

C. Research & Intellectual Capabilities

❒ Outstanding ❒ Excellent ❒ Good

❒ Satisfactory ❒ Unsatisfactory ☐

D. Industry Interface

❒ Outstanding ❒ Excellent ❒ Good

❒ Satisfactory ❒ Unsatisfactory ☐

E. Institution Building

❒ Outstanding ❒ Excellent ❒ Good

❒ Satisfactory ❒ Unsatisfactory ☐

F. Personal Attributes and Team Player Attributes
   ❐ Outstanding ❐ Excellent ❐ Good
   ❐ Satisfactory ❐ Unsatisfactory ☐

G. Overall Grading
   ❐ Outstanding ❐ Excellent ❐ Good
   ❐ Satisfactory ❐ Unsatisfactory ☐

2. Detailed remarks (To highlight strong and weak points needing special mention)

   E.g.: Strong Point: A good teacher or an inspiring personality
   Weak Point: Poor communication skills

3. Developmental measures suggested

   E.g.: • *To improve communication skills*
   • *To be more interactive in the class*

....

Signature of the Faculty (Ratee)

4. Recommendations

   (Not to be disclosed to faculty)

   May include promotion/demotion, pay hike/no hike, confirmation or extension or probation, or training abroad, etc.

....

Signature of Assessing Authority

---

5. (Remarks of the reviewing Authority)

   I do/do not concur with the above (score out 'not applicable') ....

   ....

   ....

Director/Principal

(Paras 4 and 5 are to be filled up after discussing the review process with the faculty and obtaining his signatures)

*'Do not concur' instances should be duly supported

RESEARCH, CONSULTANCY AND INDUSTRY INTERFACE

> *It is in fact nothing short of a miracle that the modern methods of instruction have not yet entirely strangled the holy curiosity of inquiry*
>
> – Albert Einstein

A major newspaper of the country has the following to say about engineering education in a particular state which has about 3 lakh seats amounting to almost one fifth of the total capacity in the country.

- 700 odd engineering colleges
- 50 percent of them more than four years old
- Majority teachers in 150 colleges are just B Tech
- About 200 colleges with less than 10 percent faculty as professors
- Poor results from first year itself

Nothing can be more indicative of the fact that teachers and their teaching skills are questionable and more pathetic is the situation where 10 colleges do not have a single PG qualified teacher while 11 colleges do not even have a single professor. NASSCOM reports say that less than 20 percent of engineering graduates are employable. The reasons for this state of affairs are well known as quality has been compromised over quantity as one well known academician had said "there are no bad students, there are only bad teachers", implying good teachers produce good students and even better citizens. With employment on their mind, B.Tech graduates generally do take up PG studies only when they do not find a worthwhile job to pursue. Correspondingly, there are even less takers for Ph D programs in engineering discipline resulting in overall shortage of qualified and talented faculty in the colleges. A rough estimate says that the present rate of producing engineering doctorates is less than 1500 per year. With almost 15 lakh engineering seats per year, and at the international average of 5 to 9% of engineering graduates getting doctorates every year, India has miles to go even to reach 1% conversion rate.

Research as an activity is a scholarly inquiry or delving deep into something to bring out a new product or a process; professionally challenging, intellectually stimulating and academically satisfying, it's an inseparable part of the teaching profession without which teaching would be lifeless. In Finland school teachers base their teaching on simple research activities they undertake on day to day basis. Somebody has rightly said that 'research is to teaching as sin is to confession, unless you participate in the former; you have little to say in the latter" (John Slaughter). We have similar sentiment echoed by Prof JG Ghosh a former Director IIT Kharagpur who told a group of teachers that teaching without research is like a stagnant pool of water which, after sometime is likely to stink. Then there is a problem of professional migration; where engineers irrespective of the discipline they pursue, either take up well paying IT jobs or go in for management studies, and as per a study both these avenues gobble up a major chunk of engineering graduates produced in the country. The left over and the rich go abroad to pursue again an altogether different field of study at PG level. The net result is a huge loss of engineering talent pool both for the engineering/manufacturing industry and the academia. With a very meager percentage of engineers taking up teaching profession, engineering colleges are finding it difficult to fulfill their basic obligations and are shying away from offering PG programs 'while the less said the better' about research/Ph D facilities, which are grossly inadequate even in some well established universities. As per a study, (Kurup and Arora) in a ten year period starting from 1998 to 2007, India has been able to produce .36 Ph D per million of population or one Ph D to teach 597 engineers at Bachelor's level and 50 engineers at Master's level, while their quality still remains debatable (V. Raghunathan). Fortunately IITs, NITs, IIITs and IISc are doing a great job in this field but their numbers are a miniscule when compared with large numbers of state run universities and colleges in the private sector. Quite in contrast, and strangely most of the research output world over comes from the universities and so are the Nobel prize winners. Thus the universities and colleges need to build a strong Research and Development eco system for the economic uplifting of the nation. If competition gets the best out of the business there is no reason why it should not do the same for research in universities and colleges. The regulatory bodies like UGC and AICTE can create centres for measuring the performance of the universities exclusively in research and apportion and allocate grants and funds accordingly (Centre for Measuring University Performance in the US). Unfortunately academia gets only 5% of the governmental R&D funding the balance going to government bodies themselves. Universities getting funds from the industry is a rarity in our country unlike elsewhere in other countries.

> *Our higher engineering institutions have severe paucity of funds leading to inadequate and ill-paid faculty, poor research facilities few research grants and non existent infrastructure quality on the campus. The situation is compounded by the fact that the industry attaches little premium to M.Techs and Doctorates. As a consequence, higher education has been reduced to accept second rate talent for admissions for Masters and Doctoral courses*
>
> – V Raghunathan in 'Is India a World Power in Engineering and Technology'

In return for good research work faculty members get recognition, promotion, pay rise, reduced teaching loads, enhanced prestige and other rewards and one time grants etc. This will give rise to increased performance which in turn will lead to higher Perceived Self Efficacy (PSE) which is defined as belief in one's ability to perform a particular task. Studies indicate that there is a positive correlation between PSE and a faculty's research output. Added to this is the institutional support in promoting research culture, research based teaching, effective faculty evaluation system, due recognition of good work and mentorship by senior faculty which are some of the other factors that motivate the faculty to take up research. This requires the colleges and universities to get and allocate adequate grants/funds and at the same time enjoy functional freedom too in deciding the salaries and incentives for the faculty undertaking research. Fortunately, many accreditation agencies have even changed their criteria to lay a much greater emphasis on large scale research in engineering education. A recent report 'Educating the Engineer of 2020 (National Academy of Engineers 2005 a. p.54) suggests that "the engineering education establishment should endorse research in engineering education as a value and rewarded activity for engineering faculty as a means to enhance and personalize the connection to undergraduate students to understand how they learn, and to appreciate the pedagogical approach that excite them" Another issue ailing the Indian engineering education system with regard to research is the teaching and evaluation methods that focus more on course coverage and knowledge dissemination than on application of knowledge, invention and investigation etc. With the result the students tend to emphasise more on marks than on getting experimental inquiry oriented. This is further corroborated by a NASSCOM – KPMG Study (2003.P.38) which quotes the observations from a World Bank Study on Science and Technology Manpower in India published in 2001 which unfortunately is as relevant today. The highlights are

- Faculty lacks industry, R&D exposure and background
- Students are not encouraged to think creatively
- Rigid curriculum is pure academics devoid of innovation and industry needs
- Teaching is purely exam oriented with no attention to problem solving skills
- No formal continuous evaluation systems
- Examinations are more memory based than on application of knowledge.

CR Swaminathan in his paper 'Research and Teaching – A Reflection on some Contemporary Issues' suggests couple of models one which depicts the essential inputs that promote good quality research in an institution of higher learning and the other as an approach for deemed universities to attract external investment support from government funding agencies, private and public sector industries and international funding agencies. They are illustrated below

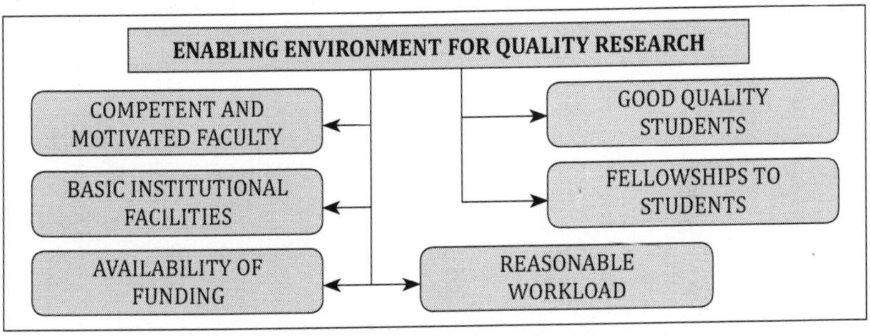

Fig. 1. Enabling Environment for Research

Source: 'Multiple Stakeholders Perspectives of Higher Education'
Ed: R Natarajan, NR Shetty: Macmillan 2012 Page 154

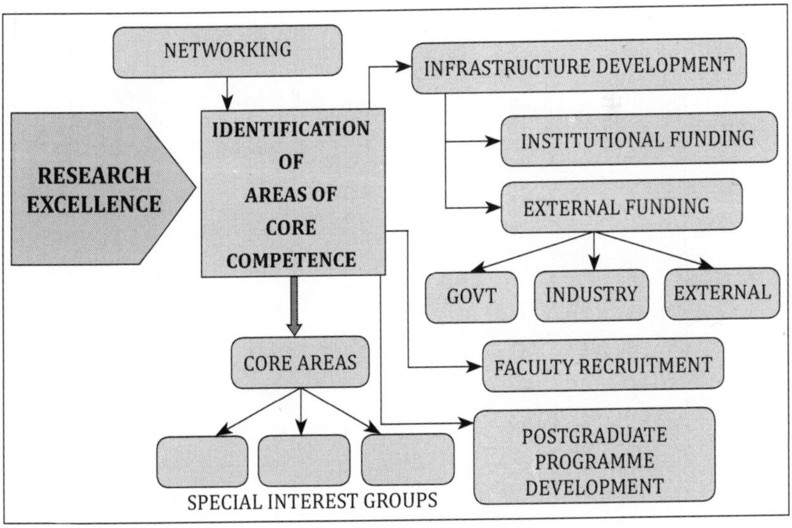

Fig. 2. A Pathway for Development of Research

Source: 'Multiple Stakeholders Perspectives of Higher Education'
Ed: R Natarajan, NR Shetty: Macmillan 2012 Page 156

There is a strong need to promote the culture of research both among students and the faculty and certain simple measures may go a long way in ensuring this. All it requires is a 'will' to do, and the right attitude on the part of the institutional head and the senior faculty. Some of them could be

- Every engineering college may be mandated to offer PG and Doctoral programs on completion of 5 years after establishment
- Provision of basic infrastructure to undertake research
- Increase PG program seats every year in various disciplines
- Increase fellowship amount for Ph D
- Get industry sponsorship for research
- Conduct Seminars on research to motivate young faculty
- Provide psychological boost to Ph D students
- Make Ph D scholars attend various seminars
- Make the teaching career more attractive
- Constitute departmental 'research committees' to encourage young faculty
- Make senior faculty to undertake 'mentorship' compulsorily
- Institute suitable mechanism to reward good work in research and quality publications
- Reduce teaching loads for Ph D scholars
- Provide adequate funds for research
- Every department to maintain a 'research topic data base' in consultation with the industry
- Regular review of research activities and close monitoring of the progress at departmental head level
- Functional freedom for research scholars to get into what is called 'flow' to achieve maximum creativity. Csikszentmihalyi(1990) describes 'flow' as the state in which people are so involved in an activity that people will do it even at great cost, for the sake of doing it.

- Ph D and PG level theses should be made available on 'open access' basis on the website of the university or that of the regulatory body

Concern for man and his destiny must always be the chief interest of all technical efforts. Never forget it in all your dreams and equations

– Albert Einstein

Prof Shyam Sundar of Yale School of Management in his commentary on 'Building Research Culture' (China Journal of Accounting Research Vol 1 Issue1 2008) suggests few simple steps to promote research culture among faculty

- People holding senior positions should have scholarly accomplishments comparable with the best in the world
- Limiting the power of hierarchy and rank over the creative younger faculty more so when those in authority are not good researchers themselves
- Encourage innovative ideas of younger faculty
- Start radically new journals
- Faculty exchange with good research institutions at minimal costs
- Linking rewards, promotion and tenure to quality research output

"It is very demanding to get Ph.D. It takes a number of years to complete and there is a tremendous number of people who start Ph Ds they never finish. It's certainly not an issue that will quickly be resolved; it's going to take the work of a lot of people to address the issue over a long period of time".

– Linda Livingstone
Dean, Pepperdine University

RESEARCH HIGHLIGHTS

- Centre for Policy Research in Higher Education (CPRHE) is being setup as an autonomous body to be funded by the Central Govt or the UGC to become a 'knowledge warehouse and a cutting edge centre of research on higher education policy". Its main objective would be to promote excellence in higher education, ensuring improved access, equity and quality

  – The Times of India, Hyderabad, Feb 02, 2012

- Dr. Mani Lal Bhaumik, the USA based physicist is setting up an advanced research centre in Kolkata with the help of IIT Kharagpur by donating 15 acres of land and raising \$150 million. The centre to be named after him is being set up with an objective of producing the next Nobel laureate from India and the noted scientist also pledged to use his personal wealth to fill any shortfall in fund raising
- A five member committee headed by Atomic Energy Commission Chairman Anil Kakodkar made its recommendations for a ten year road map for IITs this April 2012, (The Kakodkar Committee report: Taking IITs to Excellence and Greater Relevance) states that the IITs have to create an advanced research based innovation ecosystem. This needs a large pool of Ph D graduates. The best technology institutions in the world have over 15000 students as opposed to 6000 currently at each of the established IITs, the report says: USA and China produce around 8000–9000 Ph Ds in engineering technology every year. India produces 1000.
- For years now India's R & D spending has remained below 1% of GDP. In comparison, countries like China and Korea spend between 2% and 3% of GDP on R&D. Currently 80% of R&D in India is funded by the government and the rest

by industry unlike in the west where the industry is the major funder

– The Economic Times, Hyderabad, Nov 08, 2011

- Private Sector must support scientific research too. Education and research institutions must spend more time in interacting with the industry

  – NR Narayana Murthy, Chairman Emeritus, Infosys

- Most major innovations come from students. Without students there won't be great science. And without good teachers there won't be good students. That's clean. Appropriate teachers in educational institutions should be indentified and sent to research institutions so that they may become experts and teach their students. Teachers in educational institutions should teach through their own examples. Students should be exposed to good teachers, good scientists and successful people. Students need to interact and spend time with them so that they develop a scientific mentality

  – Dr Baldev Raj, Former Director
  Indira Gandhi Centre for Atomic Research, Kalpakkam

- TT Ram Mohan a professor in IIM Ahmedabad highlights the fact that the American Universities have become engines of growth, producing research that drives new industries and products. UIRCs (University Industry Research Centres) have been established with universities getting in the forefront of innovation themselves

  – The Economic Times, Hyderabad, Feb 02, 2012

- Intel's R&D centre in Bengaluru delivered the world's first terascale experimental chip capable of one trillion operations per second

  – The Atlantic Monthly, Nov 12, 2011

- Students from a city based engineering college (KMIT) won The Great Mind Challenge 2010 a nation wide software development and research contest organized by IBM India. Their project attempts to make on line banking transactions simpler and safer

  – The Hindu, Hyderabad, Nov 16, 2011

- Universitas 21, a leading global network of research universities ranks India at 48 in higher education parameter list among top 50 countries of the world, on the basis of resources per student available, research output, environment and connectivity

  – The Economic Times, Hyderabad, May 23, 2012

CONSULTANCY

What research is to teaching, consultancy is to research among the faculty. Blake and Mouton in their preface to a book "Consultation" observe "consultation and education are two most important influences behind the forward movement of society. In certain respects consultation is even more important than education in giving the society its forward thrust". The reason is simple, consultation deals with live problems on the ground while education is all about learning the theoretical academic concepts. Unfortunately in our country the practice of consultancy by the engineering faculty is mostly limited to those top notch institutions like IITs, NITs and BITS etc. IIT Bombay is reportedly handling Rs.40 million worth of consultancy assignments per year. National Foundation for Indian Engineers (NAFEN), a professional body encourages engineering faculty to take up various consultancy assignments. Consultancy as a knowledge enhancing exercise by the engineering faculty is still at a nascent stage in India with less than 10% faculty even from IITs taking it up. Despite the dwindling governmental funding, the state run universities or institutions of higher learning failed to tap their revenue generating sources through consultancy etc while America's universities saw the opportunity to augment their revenues through consulting assignments. This also helped the good research oriented faculty to earn handsome income which by itself became yet another motivating factor, for attracting and retaining them (TT Ram Mohan 2012).

INDUSTRY INTERFACE

There is no denial of the fact that the industry is a major stakeholder in the field of engineering education as it absorbs the output of the institutions in terms of the students churned out. It is imperative that these students when they join the industry become productive and become a part of the growth process. Despite this vital need the 'partners in progress' the academia and the industry tend to shy away from each other, mainly because both of them generally confine themselves to their comfort zones, rarely making an effort to get to know each other. Institutions restrict themselves to academic research only while applied research is what is being looked at by the industry, as they want their problems to be solved and not mere enhancement of knowledge per se. It's a situation where both the partners must traverse their respective distances and meet each other half way through. UIRCs (University Industry Research Centres) established in America have tremendously boosted the industry institute relationship and the US Congress went to the extent of passing an act in 1981 that allowed the universities to patent research so developed. Thus the number of patents issued to universities increased from under 400 in 1980 to 1100 in 1990 with the corresponding rise in UIRCs from 250 in 1983 to over a 1000 in 1990.

The industry in our country has a perennial grouse that engineering graduates are hardly employable and those employed rarely meet the industry's expectations unless they are trained for a considerable period at a very heavy cost. Hence it is all the more necessary and relevant that both of them meet each other at regular intervals where one specifies his need, the other makes a sincere effort to meet it, given the rigid regulatory constraints our institutions function under. To start with, the existing cultural differences between the partners need to be ironed out as academia always asserts itself as an information giver while industry insists on issue resolving attitude (Brinberg & Hirschman 1986; Cornelissen 2000). A kind of 'win-win' situation needs to be created as the industry looks to generate profits from the work of the academia while the institutions look forward to build up their intellectual property base, a fact which is echoed in the words of Desmond Hellmann who said 'when an important discovery is made at a university, scientists want to continue asking and answering questions. In contrast industry wants to finish answering questions and sell it". Yet another area of dispute between both the partners is the confidentiality of the research work and the output where the academia believes in its openness and sharing while the companies want it to be a secret in view of the economic gains they plan to derive from.

Numbers of authors have delved diligently into various aspects of Industry-Institute Interface in case of engineering colleges (Technical Education Current Status and Future Directions, Vol II, Icfai Books, The IUP 2005, by Prof R Natarajan, Engineering Education in India, Draft Final Report, IIT Bombay 2007 by Rangan Banerjee and Vinayak P. Muley and 'Profile of Engineering Education in India, Status, Concerns and Recommendations: Narosa Publishing House Pvt. Ltd, 2010 by Gautam Biswas, KL Chopra, CS Jha and DV Singh). However as we look at it from the HRM angle as a motivating factor for the faculty the following issues deserve serious attention by both the parties.

- Projects of industry relevance at bachelor, masters and Ph D levels to be taken up with industry sponsorship
- Faculty to get industry oriented by working alongside students while supervising the projects
- Regular conduct of conferences, workshops and seminars

and exchange of ideas, projecting views and requirements of each other

- Industry to sponsor their staff to undertake PG courses and Ph D programs. Institutions may also nominate their faculty for a brief tenure in the industry to seek the practical knowledge pertaining to his discipline
- Both the partners must look at their relationship as an investment portfolio
- Establish Industry Interface Cells (IICs) in the colleges by revamping the existing placement cells and increasing their scope of interaction with the industry. America's University Industry Research Centres (UIRCs) or CEUs (Continuous Education Units) could be benchmarked
- Industry to give equal importance to knowledge generation and dissemination and shed its over emphasis on profits. Likewise academia should play more proactive role in responding to the critical needs of the industry
- In view of rapid technological changes Universities must review their course curriculum at least once in two years (if not every year) to be in tune with the industry's requirements of manpower
- Colleges to maintain research data banks prepared as per the needs of the industry
- Industry representatives to form part of the advisory/ governing boards of the institutions
- Encouraging faculty and students coming up with innovative and useful products by giving them suitable incentives and awards
- Academicians to shed their 'I know enough, touch me not and Ivory Tower' image, and industry to change its attitude and mind set towards teaching profession per se
- Industry must loosen its purse strings in providing funds for the academia for research, consultancy projects and for establishing chairs etc.

Finally it is needless to say that the interaction bonds strengthen more on social platforms and both the parties must explore avenues for the same. Research adds to the knowledge base of the faculty while consultancy and industry interface have an additional feature of getting extra income for him and all of them are motivating factors by themselves for any teaching professional.

RETENTION STRATEGIES

In these days of intense competition even among education sector, retention of talent is a perennial problem more so when demand for quality faculty far exceeds the supply. Though compensation or the money still continues to be the single largest motivator but surprisingly that is not the only reason as to why faculties shift from one college to another. As the educational institutions are also getting corporatized, an often repeated corridor remark 'people quit their bosses, not their job" may apply equally to academia too. A leader's job is to motivate his team to perform well and exceed the expectations by each passing day and an educational institution's head's job is no different in this regard. Teachers being very sensitive by nature tend to have more psychological or self esteem needs than physical ones. Any compromise on this aspect is likely to wean them away from the organizational objectives or their own for that matter. Having discussed these issues adequately in the HR cycle, which started with acquisition consisting of recruitment and selection, continued with development through training, and touching upon the major issues of motivation, the process culminates in retaining the faculty so nurtured so far. The cycle starts with appointing a faculty at the appropriate level consistent with their academic accomplishments and experience. Mentoring is yet another important aspect of motivating a junior faculty to stay. Formalizing this, is the need of the hour. Nobody who is averse to learning takes up teaching profession. Faculty development programs help the junior faculty to learn and the senior faculty to learn and earn at the same time by being the resource persons, and both the activities are motivating factors to the respective groups. Campuses may also institute mechanisms to address special needs of the faculty in terms of transport, schooling facility for children, medical care, flexible working hours, special leave for research or for undertaking projects and consultancy assignments etc. Pay parity is of critical significance in retaining the faculty. Of all, creating a conducive campus climate is the most vital element of the faculty retention strategy for any educational institution, more so for an engineering college as quality and good faculty are rare commodities these days. Certain measures that are likely to help the institutional heads are

- Entire faculty to get involved in all student related activities both curricular and co curricular as against limiting it to few interested ones only. This strengthens the bond between faculty and student and between faculty and the institution
- Making cabin consultations between students and faculty a regular feature of academic delivery
- Providing academic freedom, and encouraging innovation in teaching
- Terms of employment should ensure job security, be financially rewarding, while granting fair balance between work and personal life
- Personal and professional development needs of the faculty must be addressed
- Institute, 'best teacher' and 'role model' and 'long service' awards for faculty
- Quality infrastructure and quality students, both lead to passionate teaching by the faculty
- Industry interaction through seminars, consultancy, projects and workshops to be made a routine in the colleges
- Instituting an effective 'feedback' mechanism (format at Annexure VI to this chapter)

- Conducting 'exit' interviews compulsorily and addressing the grey areas that get manifested therein
- Recognize and reward the merit and hard work on 'instantaneous' basis
- Assign an important role in institution building activity
- Sending faculty abroad on faculty exchange programs
- Ensuring appropriate role (commensurate with their position) in academic decision making process
- Periodic social interactions between teaching, non teaching staff, their family members and students
- Maintain effective linkages with the past/retired faculty through 'newsletters' and alumni get togethers
- **Finally a suitable HR functionary should be put in place to take care of all HR needs of the faculty on a proactive basis**

  (*Let us not forget the fact "in hell there is no retention"* Miguel de CS)

Concluding Remarks

'People are different' is the basic HR principle and as such they have different needs. Motivating faculty, and maintaining their morale is an intricate and sensitive subject. Institutional heads need to be aware of variety of motivational needs of their faculty (which also change over time), and address them accordingly. This understanding of the faculty motivation process requires a carefully designed and systematic approach where in the 'feedback' from the faculty forms an essential part.

> *Our assets walk out of the door each evening.*
> *We have to make sure that they come back the next morning.*
>
> – Mr. Narayana Murthy, Chairman Emeritus, Infosys

Annexure VI

FEED BACK FORM

(To be discussed definitely during Exit Interview)

(**Note:** This form may be filled up by faculty either during service or while separating from the institute)

1. Designation: .... 2. Date of Joining: ....
3. Present CTC ₹: .... 4. Expected CTC ₹: ....
5. Comment on working environment/organizational culture.

   ____

   ____

   ____

6. Comment on your relationship with your boss
   (a) Do you receive appreciation for your good work (Y/N)
   (b) Are you treated well (Y/N)
   (c) Are you listened to – (Y/N)
   (d) Do you receive coaching and guidance? (Y/N)
   (e) Does the work stimulate and challenge you? (Y/N)
   (f) Do you feel discriminated (Y/N)

7. Comment on the learning, development, promotional avenues

   ____

   ____

8. Specific Reasons for leaving the organization (other than mentioned above)

   ____

   ____

9. Do you consider coming back at a later date – Yes/No?
   If No, elaborate

   ____

10. Have you enjoyed your work and interaction with students – Yes/No?
    If No, elaborate

    ____

11. Any other comments/suggestions you would like to make for the general improvement of the organization

    ____

    ____

    ____

    ____

Date ____________ Signature ____________

Name ______________

Dept. ______________

9

Leadership and Governance

I start with the premise that the function of leadership is to produce more leaders not more followers

– Ralph Nader

LEADERSHIP

Leadership is the art of influencing people towards achievement of goals. In case of an educational institution, it is the key to transform the students, the faculty and the society at large. Leaders are neither born nor made but the capacity to lead is inherent in every human being and all it requires is the right environment to manifest. Engineers are going to shape the industrial rather the economic destiny of the nation; hence the leadership of engineering colleges producing these very engineers assumes critical significance. Students tend to form their notions, values, beliefs and base their ethical behavior from what they learn, see, feel and experience both inside and outside the class room of an institution, as leadership by example is the most effective form of leadership.

Well known management teacher and institutional builder J Philip in his paper 'Leadership and Excellence in Higher Education' succinctly highlights the issues concerning the higher educational institutions in our country. Briefly they are

- Qualitative (software) aspects like people, culture and creativity are more important than 'quantitative' (hardware) like infrastructure etc

- Excellent institutions must differentiate themselves from the 'also ran' types in terms of students' satisfaction, their quality and value in the market, internal climate of the institution, quality and quantity of intellectual/ professional output, and finally adding further value to the value addition process itself
- Striving for and achieving excellence to become an essential feature of the institution
- Leadership, people, culture and shared values are the most important aspects for any institution

Our 'leadership' in particular the revered management guru opines that a large number of institutional heads function more as 'caretakers' rather than as 'builders', generally maintaining the 'status quo'. Fundamental issue here is of choosing the right person for the job, where the practice is to hire some one for being a good teacher, a researcher with number of publications to his credit etc but with no consideration for managerial, operational or administrative experience. This glaring gap in the criteria forces the incumbent in either giving up or towing the line or just marking his time invariably putting the institution on a downward path. He identifies the following essential attributes for an institutional leader

- A visionary and a good manager
- A strong Leader – could be less of a teacher or a researcher
- An excellent change manager and networker
- A perfect line-staff integrator
- Pursue excellence over elitism
- An innovator, and a right culture builder
- Growth oriented

Engineering faculty have multiple roles to play like teaching, research, consultancy, admin/managerial, participation in activities of professional societies/bodies and continuing education activities etc (R Natarajan 2005) apart from institution building activities.

Only those teachers who have successfully carried out the above functions, over a period of two to three decades, and carved a niche for themselves are considered for leadership positions to head the institutions. However, while picking up a leader apart from the above 'eligibility' related factors, one needs to seriously consider the 'suitability' parameter too which relates to the ability of producing results irrespective of the situation one is in. Unfortunately this criteria is generally overlooked and most of the engineering colleges specially those in the private sector (barring a few) are leaving a lot to be desired in ensuring sound operations and proper management of their institutions which is reflecting in the poor employability of the engineers produced. Despite the odds in terms of lack of support from the sponsoring body or shortage of funds an effective leader with his ' where there is a will ....' attitude can still pursue his twin goals of proper knowledge dissemination and churning out good citizens for the country. Research proved that an educational institution is akin to a business enterprise in delivering results and it has also been proved by research that only one third university staff had confidence in their leader as far as his HR abilities and people management skills are concerned. That is to say, any faculty aspiring to become an institutional leader needs to nurture his administrative, operational, managerial and people management capabilities too.

Institutional leaders need to be self aware (an ability to know self and impact on others), possess deep senses of integrity, commitment and empathy, be a store of house knowledge and skill in a chosen area, highly demanding and finally be a developer of more leaders. He can be effective by setting personal examples, in terms of publishing, handling an occasional interactive session with students (no harm in handling a regular course: many do it) having deep concern for the welfare of the faculty, admin staff and of the students by resorting to active listening, taking criticism in right spirit avoiding vindictiveness, (generally noticed) and having a full control on finances and the budget are few other attributes which are equally important for an institutional leader. Further it is needless to say that he has to take his team along, be a sound planner, an articulate visionary, able to manage crisis, a consensus builder, possess PR skills, maintain transparency in all dealings, trust others and be trusted, industry oriented and finally be a staunch disciplinarian. (Discipline is the heart and soul of an educational institution). It is through these intellectual and transformational attributes, combined with their charisma and inspiration, institutional leaders provide a clear sense of purpose and mission to their faculty and students.

> *The principal goal of education is to create men who are capable of doing things, not simply of repeating what other generations have done*
>
> – Jan Piaget (Swiss Psychologist)

GOVERNANCE

> *Government will not fail to employ education, to strengthen its hands, and perpetuate its institutions*
>
> – William Godwin

India has one of the largest technical education systems in the world, but the employability of the engineers produced or the near dismal rate of engineering doctorates being churned out has always been a cause for concern. Higher Education being a part of the 'concurrent list', more often than not, with two different political parties at the centre and the state levels, the policies, the rules and regulations laid down tend to be more at divergence than at convergence resulting in a chaotic situation. No doubt the state of higher education in our country rarely receives accolades from the academics of repute. Good governance is, laying down sound rules and regulations so that institutional heads can implement them and deliver goods to the satisfaction of all the stake holders. The policies and guidelines so framed must hold the hands of the institutional heads to further their cause instead of being archaic and authoritative. We have a host of regulatory bodies both at centre and state levels and if their 'imposing' posture is replaced by 'interact and integrate' role to present a common agenda, probably the institutions may govern themselves better. As rightly brought out in the treatise. 'The Role of Engineering Education in India' (Gautam Biswas and others-2010) "a model governance framework must provide academic, administrative and financial autonomy with built in measures for checks and balances and accountability to usher in culture of *institute of academics, for academics, by academics*".

Governance is a shared responsibility between the stake holders and hence a synergetic approach is what is required. Faculty apart from handling their teaching loads must take keen interest in academic administration, students' activities, industry interface, research and publications, peer group activities, and finally in being a student and learner himself. It needs no debate that faculty have the tremendous power to transform the student community and thus the face of the society itself (*Give me a child for seven years, afterwards let God or devil take the child, they cannot change the child* – Ancient Greek Teacher).

Professional bodies have a complementary role to play in preparing the younger generation to meet the requirements of the industry. At present, they tend to keep themselves away from the academic institutions and it is essential that the latter on their own should knock on their doors and draw the professional guidance from these bodies. Engineering Council of India (ECI) is an apex body of nearly 25 professional outfits like Institution of Engineers, Institution of Electronics and Telecommunication Engineers (IETE) and Computer Society of India (CSI) etc. ECI shall play a big brother role in ensuring proper code of conduct among engineers through these societies in the respective disciplines.

Governance issues are more relevant and critical for private engineering colleges as they produce close to 85% engineers in the country today, with the affiliation to state run universities, though some of them enjoy deemed university status etc. The governing body (reportedly consisting of 12 members, sponsoring Society/ Trust-6, AICTE-1 University to which the college is affiliated -2, State Govt reps – 3) has an active role to play in ensuring proper governance of the college irrespective of the fact whether the college enjoys the 'autonomous' status or not. The investor trust/society must provide the institutional head with adequate freedom and flexibility in operations as against the normal practice of maximizing the return on investment. Quality may not cost much but it does not come cheap either. Good infrastructure in terms of technical, academic and administrative facilities and good quality faculty are going to make a substantial difference in bringing out bright engineering graduates. Fortunately the recent intense competition among private engineering colleges in the country proved to be a boon for the students and their parents as the 'quality aspects', have received a tremendous boost, and some of the private engineering colleges have risen to world class standards and they attract a large number of foreign students. The institutional head, the sponsoring society and the governing body have a sacred responsibility in nurturing the college and steer its growth through various developmental processes.

NON TEACHING STAFF

By far the most neglected staff in an educational institution are the non teaching staff. Most of them tend to serve for a long time (unlike the teaching staff who move frequently) and some of them do it for their entire life time, and it is only natural and human that students tend to remember them more fondly and affectionately over their teachers even. They normally consist of academic co-ordinators, office staff, hostel wardens, canteen staff, laboratory/workshop assistants, student counsellors, placement executives and office boys etc, and it is a fact that they have an equally important role in shaping the future of the young student for whom everybody is a teacher (formal and informal). Unknowingly they contribute to the holistic development of the student and they should be allowed and encouraged to involve themselves in healthy interactions with the student community. They form that vital link between the 'teacher and the taught' without whose support and assistance no teaching can virtually take place. They are the first to reach and the last to leave the college. Their student friendliness and helping attitude make them very popular in the campus. While the faculty being a "high demand resource" gets their due, it is this voiceless non teaching staff that are denied their rightful dues. College Heads/Governing bodies may pay special attention to the HRM needs of the non teaching staff as they do in case of teaching fraternity as discussed in the earlier chapters. Ideal would be to have a full fledged HR set up in the college with an exclusive junior HR executive solely looking into the welfare of the non teaching staff.

> *'One peculiar phenomenon of most large educational institutions is the internal mismatch between the academic and administrative sub-systems. The values and models of the two sub-systems often differ. The reasons are obvious and the cost of the phenomenon has been high. While there have been programmes and efforts to upgrade the quality of teaching sub-system, not enough has been done to upgrade or strengthen the quality of the administrative sub-system. This problem needs urgent attention so that there will be better integration, goal orientation and synergy within the system.*
>
> – J Philip

SUMMARY

Leader of an engineering college has an onerous task which may include, budgeting, public relations, planning, mediation, consultancy, staff development, articulating a vision, working on a mission, crisis management, sound operations, consensus building etc where the list is endless. Intellectual and transformational leadership skill is the basic requirement. Finally a suggested organogram of a typical engineering college in the private sector is given at Annexure I, to the chapter.

Engineering colleges of the country are like a backbone to the society and their contribution to the national economy is enormous. When the employability of the engineering graduates is becoming a matter of continuous national debate there is a strong need to deeply delve into operational issues of these colleges to critically examine the way they are managed, administered and governed. HRM of the staff particularly of the teaching fraternity is of critical importance in these days of heavy and intense competition.

> *"The challenge is to make people employable, bridge the skill deficit, and provide them with vocational training"*
>
> – S Ramadorai
> Former Vice Chairman, TCS

Annexure I

Suggested Organisational Tree of a Typical Private Engineering College

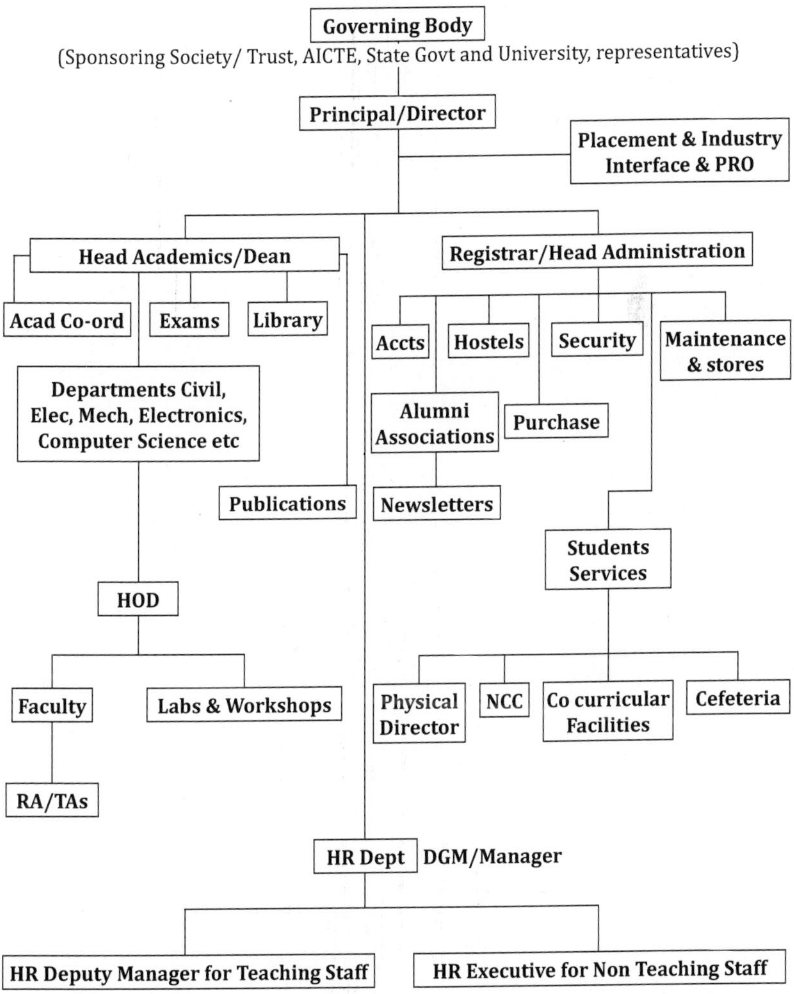

Conclusion

The main thrust of the book is to highlight the most essential need of an exclusive HR functionary/department for engineering colleges so that the staff is taken care of, and their HR related needs are adequately addressed. To that extent the effort is pioneering in its nature, while the ultimate aim is to produce 'engineers of quality' for the country.

A lot has been drawn from the well received earlier work 'The Business of HR in Business Schools' as the basic HR issues are similar for both the categories of institutions with only minor differences which have been adequately addressed. All possible efforts have been made to keep the discussions and formats very simple devoid of any heavy conceptual frameworks. Each chapter has been treated as an independent entity, so that institutional heads and faculty may find it easy to refer and implement the suggestions if considered acceptable. Hope the book meets its intended objectives.

> *We should remember that immediately on attainment of freedom our people are not going to secure happiness. As we become independent all the defects in the system of election, injustice, the tyranny of richer classes and also the burden of running administration are bound to come upon us. People will begin to feel that during those (British) days, there was more justice, there was better administration, there was peace, and there was honesty to a great extent among the administrators compared to the days after independence., But there is hope, if*

education spreads throughout the country and people develop from their childhood, qualities of pure conduct, God fearing and love. Otherwise India would become an abode of grave injustice, and tyranny of the Rulers

– Mahatma Gandhi

Bibliography

1. "Technical Education: Current Status and Future Directions" Volumes I,II and III; R. Natarajan; The Icfai University Press, Hyderabad:2005
2. The Times of India, Hyderabad Oct 31, 2011
3. The Hindu, Hyderabad, Nov 02, 2011
4. The Times of India, Hyderabad, Jan 10, 2011
5. The Business of HR in Business Schools: Dr VRK Prasad Viva Books Pvt Ltd, New Delhi, 2011
6. 'The Need for Proper HR Practices in Education' Mysore/ Deccan Herald.com/ 15th Apr 2009
7. The Atlantic Monthly Nov 12,2011 "India: The World's Secret Silicon Valley"
8. The Economic Times, Hyderabad, Nov 15, 2011
9. "Education Sector: HR Perspectives": VRK Prasad (Ed): Volumes I & II(Resp): The Icfai University Press, Hyderabad 2006 and 2007
10. Working for a Noble Cause: Ahona Ghosh "The Economic Times, Hyderabad Nov 08, 2011
11. http://www.namstct.org/ADB_RETA_Report/Prof_KL_Chopra_Prof_PBsharma.pdf
12. Handbook on Engineering Education 2008: Association of Indian Universities, New Delhi Publication Eleventh Edition 2008

13. Engineering Education in India Draft Final Report by Rangan Banerjee, and Vinayak P Muley sponsored by Observer Research Foundation for Energy Systems Engineering, IIT Bombay Powai, Mumbai, Sep 14 2007 (Source: www.ese.iitb.ac.in/EnEdu.pdf)

14. The Hindu, Hyderabad, Nov 17,2011

15. Profile of Engineering Education in India: Status Concerns and Recommendations: Gautam Biswas, KL Chopra, CS Jha, DV Singh: Narosa Publishing House Pvt. Ltd, New Delhi 2010 (Source:www.inae.org/book/Profilebook.pdf)

16. Deccan Chronicle, Hyderabad, Nov 16, 2011

17. Engineering Education (India) (http://wiki.ask.com/Engineering-education)

18. Engineering Education in India: A story of Contrast(http://www.wes.org/ewenr/07jan/feature.htm)

19. All India Council for Technical Education from Wikipedia the free encyclopedia (http://en.wikipedia.org/wiki/ALL_India_Council_for_Technical_Education)

20. Competency focused Engineering Education with Reference to IT Relative Disciplines: is the Indian System Ready for Transformation?-Sanjay Goel: Journal of Information Technology Education Volume 5,2006 (http://iite.org/documents/vol5/v5p027-052Goel88.pdf)

21. EIA Curriculum in Engineering Courses in India: Review of Effectiveness, Challenges and Opportunities-Indra N Sinha (http://www.penta.eu.net/docs/Indra_Nath_Sinha-EIA.curriculum.pdf)

22. The Times of India, Hyderabad Nov 16, 2011 ('Ideate and Innovate' by Jitendra Malik and Pankaj Jalote)

23. The Hindu, Hyderabad Nov 16, 2011

24. The Sunday Indian Jul 10, 2011

25. The Economic times, Hyderabad, Nov 08, 2011

26. The Week June 05, 2011
27. India Today Jul 18, 2011
28. Outlook, June 27, 2011
29. Contemporary Issues in Engineering Education –Edited buy R. Natarajan, MP Ravindra, and R Hariharn Macmillan Publishers India Ltd, 2008
30. XXI Century Priorities in Engineering Education –Edited by R Natarajan, and M Ananda Krishnan: Macmillan Publishers 2010.
31. Deccan Chronicle, Hyderabad, Nov 27, 2011
32. The Hindu, Hyderabad, Nov 30, 2011
33. The Economic Times, Hyderabad, Dec 13 and 16, 2011
34. Mint,Hyd Dec 20,2011
35. Sunday Times of India, Hyd, Jan 22, 2012
36. The times of India, Hyd, Feb 02, 2012
37. The Economic Times, Hyd, Feb 02, 2012
38. The Deccan Chronicle, Hyd, Feb 04, 2012
39. The Hindu, Hyderabad, Mar 14, 2012
40. The Hindu, Hyderabad, Mar 21, 2012
41. Business Manager May 2012 (Integrating Academia and Industry: Challenges Ahead: Dr. Nidhi Maheshwari)
42. Motivation as a Retention Strategy- Ed PSV Ramana, VV Ramani, Icfai Books, The IUP, 2009
43. The Economic Times, Hyderabad May 23, 2012
44. International Accreditation Perspectives, Ed – R Natarajan, Macmillan Publishers India Ltd, 2012 (An ISTE Publication)
45. Multiple stakeholder perspectives of Higher Education, Ed- R. Natarajan, NR Shetty, Macmillan Publishers India Ltd, 2012, (An ISTE Publication)
46. The Hindu, Hyderabad, May 30, 2012

47. www.rediff.comhttp://www.rediff.com/getahead/slide-show/slide-show-1-career-indias-best-engineering-college-2012/20120531.htm

48. www.pccoepune.com/mech/doc/31_DrVPGosavi.doc

49. The Decan Chronicle, Hyderabad, June 18, 2012

50. The Times of India, Hyderabad, June 06, 2012

51. Sunday Times of India, Hyderabad, June 17, 2012

52. The Hindu, Hyderabad, July 27, 2012

53. www.rediff.com, July 25, 2012: A report by Aspiring Minds

54. The Enigma of Indian Engineering by James Trevelyan The Hindu, Hyderabad, June 20, 2012

55. 'Our IITs have a lot to catchup' by V Sethuraman and 'Engineers are not the end Product' by Ravi Kumar Tadepalli The Hindu, Hyderabad, July 15, 2012

56. The Deccan Chronicle, Hyderabad, June 30, 2012

57. The Deccan Chronicle, Hyderabad, Aug 08, 2012

58. The Deccan Chronicle, Hyderabad, Aug 17, 2012